12

THE YORKS

What they said about Paul Ingle:

'An excellent fighter, a good champion and a great guy. He was a very special talent and showed that against Naz. At a time when Naz was invincible, Paul caused him a lot of problems and was unlucky to lose. One of them was going to run out of steam and he was unlucky it was him...'

- Joe Calzaghe

'Paul's work-rate was immense. He was called the Yorkshire Hunter for a reason! When he had somebody on the back foot, he wouldn't let them off the hook with his power and energy...'

- Billy Hardy

'A true Yorkshireman through and through. If you looked up Yorkshire Terrier in the dictionary there should be a picture of Paul Ingle there. He was in it for the game not the fame...'

- Johnny Nelson

'Every time he won a new title, he would become the first featherweight British champ, then first Commonwealth etc in Scarborough. Everything he did came with a headline. He re-wrote history every time he stepped in the ring and the people in the local area loved him for that. Especially as he never wanted to move away. They were loyal to him – he repaid that loyalty at every opportunity he could.

'A gritty, fiery, determined, tough individual, who would always give better than his best every time he stepped into the ring...'

- Glenn McCrory

'Winning two world titles that day in the boxing mecca of the United States has to be the pinnacle for any champion...'

- IBO President, Ed Levine

'I've sparred with a number of world champions and I can honestly say he's one of the most down-to-earth and likeable people to have ever worn a world title belt. To have become a friend of his is something very special to me.

'A true world champion and a humble guy inside and outside of the ring. Even if I try hard, I can't think of a bad thing to say about the fella...'

- Graham Earl

'I have always had a soft spot for Paul Ingle. A true fighter through his career, and an even braver fighter after it. Paul always had a wonderful sense of humour and was a pleasure to interview. Still has, and still is. A world class boxing man through and through...'

- Adam Smith

'He shouldn't be remembered for what happened at the end of his career, he should be remembered for what he achieved during it. He was an incredible fighter...'

- Robin Reid

'What a warrior, what an under-rated warrior Ingle was. Paul was a throwback, he would hunt you down, chase you all night and thrill those who'd paid to watch the brutal little man at work...'

- Tris Dixon, Boxing News *Editor*

THE YORKSHIRE HUNTER

My Autobiography

Paul Ingle

Scratching Shed Publishing Ltd

Cover image: Paul Ingle celebrates beating Junior Jones with
a TKO in the eleventh round of their IBF Featherweight
Championship fight on Saturday 29 April 2000 at Madison
Square Garden, New York ©AP/PA

Every effort has been made to trace the copyright holders
of images used. Any oversight will be rectified in future
editions at the earliest opportunity by the publishers.

A catalogue record for this book is available from the
British Library.

Typeset in Warnock Pro Semi Bold and Palatino
Printed and bound in the United Kingdom by
Charlesworth Press, Flanshaw Way, Flanshaw Lane,
Wakefield, WF2 9LP

To my mother and my late uncles,
George and Alec

Double act: Paul Zanon and Paul Ingle.

Acknowledgements - I

I NEVER really wanted to have my book written, simply because, after the accident, my life was a blur. I didn't feel comfortable with talking about it as I hadn't come to grips with things myself. However, when Sonny Pollard mentioned about doing it in 2013, the time felt right. I was starting to get my life back together and my focus and enthusiasm was also much better. I'm so glad I finally did it.

Having the chance to relive some of the best moments of my boxing career has been outstanding and to do it with some of the people who have meant so much to me over the years has made me appreciate my journey that bit more. One which they have made me realise is not over yet.

I owe massive thanks to everyone who took the time to dish some dirt on me and for helping to jog some great memories. My mum, my brother Dean, Leanne and all my uncles, aunts and cousins especially.

Outside of my family, Steve Collins, Chris Hooper, Mick Williamson, the team at Sky (Adam Smith, Johnny Nelson, Ed Robinson, Glenn McCrory), Robin Reid, Colin Dunne, Sonny Pollard, Steve Pollard, Ronnie Brown, Tris Dixon, Kenny Brocklehurst, Lee Stephenson, Sandra Cooke,

John and Dawn Amos, Graham Earl, Neil Featherby, Junior Jones, Colin McMillan, Joe Calzaghe, IBO President Ed Levine, Spencer Oliver, Ian Irwin, Tommy Johnson, Kellie Maloney (thanks for the great foreword), Billy Hardy, Rocky Rowe, Peter Richardson, George Rhodes, Franny Norton, Mark Legge, Kevin Cowley, Luca Rosi and three of my best mates – Daz Smith, Neil Cox and Wayne Smith.

Last but not least, the man who performed my life saving operation, Mr Robert Battersby.

The *Scarborough News*, *Hull Daily Mail* and Simon Baxter for their continued support and royalty-free photography. Daniel Gregory, particularly, has been a rock, following my every movement over the last couple of years, always eager to update the public on my progress. James Smailes and Dick Tingle have also been an excellent source of information and guidance and are two of Yorkshire's finest gentlemen. My gratitude too goes to Mike Tyas for his invaluable help with the proofreading.

To everyone at Scarborough ABC for never shutting the door on me. You always left it open and that has certainly been an inspirational reason for me to want to still be involved in the sport I love. Thank you.

I got to know Paul Zanon through my great friend Sonny, who said he would help me write my autobiography, detailing my life and career. I met him over a year ago now and from that first moment, I felt as though I had known him all my life. I really could not have asked for a nicer bloke to help me write this book. He has worked so hard and helped me through this tough time. He has not just become a very true friend but is like part of the family. I cannot thank him enough for all he has done for me and I hope we will spend many more, happy times with each other. Thank you again Paul.

Paul Ingle, February 2015

Acknowledgements - II

FIRST and foremost I'd like to thank a lady who has been as inspirational as the Yorkshire Hunter himself. Carol Ingle's willingness to ensure her son's story was told as accurately and clearly as possible was always at the forefront of her mind. When this Londoner walked through their door, I was immediately welcomed with a warm reception and an abundance of hospitality. I certainly never went thirsty or hungry at the Ingle household.

Thank you Carol, my time spent with you over the last year has taught me many lessons in life.

I am indebted to all the people who have spent time sharing their anecdotes. Without you, the book would lack depth and reasoning. I'd like to specifically mention a few lads who have been there for any of my late night emails or texts asking little questions about the champ, or confirmation that what I was including was accurate.

Daz Smith, Neil Cox, Wayne Smith and Dean Ingle - you are absolute gentlemen and I'll never forget the six hour 'research session' we did at the pub down Falsgrave. Well, I remember the first four hours anyway! You have made me appreciate true Scarborough hospitality.

Last but not least, I'd like to thank Paul Ingle.

Not for having given me the incredible opportunity of walking in his shoes and writing his life story, but for being a genuine role model. His sense of humour, massive heart and determination throughout our time together has been priceless. You've taught me that whatever stage you are in life, whatever it throws at you, you can always come back.

Best of all I have made a friend for life and that's the most precious thing I'll take away from having helped write your story.

Paul Zanon, February 2015

★ ★ ★ **Fight Card** ★ ★ ★

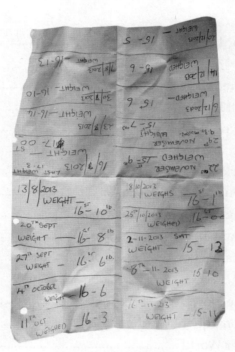

Piece of paper: Paul Ingle's weight diary.

Foreword

☐

Kellie Maloney

'THE IBF AND NOW IBO FEATHERWEIGHT CHAMPION OF THE WOOOOORRLD, PAAAAAUL INNNNNNNGLE'

That night at Madison Square Garden on the 29 April 2000 was, without doubt, one of the best of my life. I had three fighters on the card but it was Paul's contest that grabbed the attention. Although Lennox Lewis was the headliner – he knocked Michael Grant out in two one-sided rounds – Paul's bout had all the drama of a movie. Going out there as the underdog, fighting in Junior Jones's backyard and getting knocked down in the ninth round, to then come back and stop him had everyone on the edge of their seats. It was a scorcher.

The flight home was also pretty memorable too. The atmosphere from the second we boarded was brilliant. A member of the crew announced us to the other passengers and, as we sat down, the reception we got was like being back at Madison Square Garden. We were showered with anything we wanted for the rest of the flight and it was the first time in my life I'd ever been absolutely legless on an aeroplane.

The Yorkshire Hunter

****

WHEN I first started in boxing, I promoted a guy called Steve Pollard, who was probably one of the best journeyman fighters I'd ever come across. Years later, in 1993, Steve contacted me and said, 'I've got this young kid who wants to go pro and I'm going to train him. He's looking for someone to manage and promote him. His name's Paul Ingle and I think he's going to be a world champion.'

I remember watching Paul as an amateur, fighting at the Olympics and winning the ABA title twice and thought to myself, 'This kid's got talent – serious talent'. I decided to invite him to the Lennox Lewis-Frank Bruno fight in Cardiff, so we could discuss a plan which would map out the first couple of years of his pro career. We had a good chat, watched Lennox win and the following morning we shook hands and the deal was cemented.

In under three years from the time of turning pro, Paul beat respected former world champion Colin McMillan and became British featherweight champion. The fight was great and the celebration after was immense, as the Yorkshire Hunter and his crazy following all piled into a pub I'd hired out in Petticoat Lane. We partied hard into the early hours and I cherish those memories dearly.

Two years later, I'd managed to get Paul a crack at the IBF world crown against the tough Mexican, Manuel Medina. Unfortunately, I couldn't see the fight live because I was out in Las Vegas for the Lennox Lewis-Evander Holyfield rematch. I did however convince the Sky crew in Vegas to allow me to watch it in the back of one of their trucks. The noise I could hear from his supporters and the nerves I was feeling watching the fight on television made me feel like I was in Hull. As with many of Paul's top level championship fights, he was often the underdog and, as such, he pretty much always proved everyone wrong.

He gave me an almighty scare in the last few seconds of the final round when he went down, but once the bell went and the decision was announced that he was the new world champion, I was jumping up and down inside that truck like a madman screaming, 'You did it, you did it!'

I was so hyped up for Paul's fight that by the time Lennox and Holyfield fought later that night I was mentally and physically drained; I'd already peaked with excitement.

I travelled to Scarborough as quickly as I could afterwards to congratulate Paul and Steve Pollard. I knew Scarborough Council were putting on a celebration but the open-top bus parade they had lined up for him blew away everyone's expectations. It was like England had won the World Cup. There was a sea of people down every street and the cheers for Paul were relentless. I'm not sure Scarborough will ever celebrate that way for anyone ever again.

Paul was a promoter's dream. He had a certain way about him – almost a boy next door image. He was loved by everyone back home, didn't trash talk and was always very respectful to all his opponents. His story and raise to fame was like a fairy tale. He was one of three fighters who I'd taken from initial signature to the ultimate goal in the profession of boxing. He was a very special talent.

He was also very respectful to me, especially when I was not perfect. Due to my dyslexia, I've always had problems in pronouncing names and I've always referred to him as Paul 'Ingles', instead of 'Ingle'. He often corrected me, but never publicly, which I really did appreciate. He hated bullies and would never take a cheap shot at anybody inside or outside of the ring.

The saddest night ever in boxing for me, was the one in Sheffield when Paul fought Mbulelo Botile in December 2000. In my own mind I knew Paul wasn't right for the fight. It just felt there was something missing but I didn't know what and I probably never will. It wasn't the Paul who stepped in to the ring in Hull against Manuel Medina or in Madison Square Garden against Junior Jones to become a double world champion.

Since the accident I've never felt the same about boxing. I'd even go as far as to say that it was the start of me falling out of love with the sport. I'd seen other fighters get injuries and had always found a way to deal with it, but I couldn't deal with Paul's. It took over me.

I'm so glad he's now back in the sport as a mentor. I genuinely know that he still has a lot to offer to boxing. He's still an ambassador for it and he's got incredible knowledge.

Paul will always be a friend and remembered as a great boxing champion. My front door will always be open to him. It's been an honour to be asked to write the foreword to his autobiography and I hope it achieves the success it deserves.

Kellie Maloney (formerly Frank)
Paul Ingle's Manager and Promoter

The
YORKSHIRE
HUNTER

Seconds out...

Round 1

☐

A Different Sort of Fight

ALTHOUGH it was the eleventh round, I felt so fresh; 10 times fresher than in the Medina and Naz fights.

Even before the bell went, I was off my stool, not just to show Jones I still had energy left but because I wanted to get out there and finish it.

About 15 seconds in, I caught him with a massive straight right, the very same attack I'd been successful with in the second round.

As I followed up with a jab, he almost fell over and I sensed my chance. With him jammed in the corner, I unloaded a flurry of punches, not so much style as quantity, until the ref stepped between us and told me to stop punching.

My fans were going crazy, they thought I'd won but then the ref, Steve Smoger, shocked everyone – he started a standing count, which was not allowed under the rules.

I couldn't believe what I was seeing, especially as Steve was very well respected at his job. Short of throwing a few punches back on Junior's behalf, he was doing everything he could to keep him in the fight.

As soon as the count was done, I jumped straight back on him and he tried to hold on but stumbled to the floor.

In the meantime, I suddenly realised I'd picked up a cut over my right eye which was streaming down the side of my face.

As much as Jones tried to hold on for the next 30 seconds, I kept pushing him off and when the opportunity came for me to pounce on him in the corner again, the ref did the right thing and stood in front of him and waved it off this time. Minutes later I was being hailed by the legendary ring announcer Michael Buffer as a dual Featherweight champion of the world.

What music to my ears.

Junior was very gracious in defeat, gave me a hug and congratulated me. He would later go on to say, 'When I had him down I thought that was it! But he got up, rode the storm, fought back hard and put us back into a hell of a fight. Madison Square Garden had a treat tonight.' I was grateful to him for that.

Eventually watching it back, Ian Darke on Sky mentioned, 'He's going to become a star here in the US. They're going to love Ingle with his style of boxing.'

I was on top of the world, it seemed everyone was talking about me.

I'd already had the American's attention from when I fought Naz on HBO but now, with a couple more big pay days with the right opponents, I could not only retire, but retire a millionaire.

****

Three months had passed by since I lost my world titles and almost my life.

A Different Sort of Fight

As I limped to the bathroom to look in a mirror, I saw the scar on the side of my head and noticed it was in the shape of a big question mark.

It was like a constant reminder of my frustration of not understanding why I couldn't do everything as I used to and trying to work out why this happened to me in the first place.

Although physically I was managing better week by week, mentally I was all over the place.

For some reason my brain was telling me that I was still living with my mum at her house. Every now and then I'd stand up in my own home and shout, 'I don't live here. What am I doing here? I'm going back home.'

Even if somebody asked me my home address, I'd give them my mum's – which I hadn't lived at since 1998.

I felt disorientated in what I thought were unfamiliar surroundings. To top it off, when my fiancée was round, I didn't recognise her.

I remember calling my mum from the toilet once, talking in a soft voice, worried that 'this girl' in the house could hear me talking about her. My memory had pushed me back so far that I thought I was going out with someone else.

In my mind, I decided I wanted to drive home and asked her for the car keys.

I could see the look on her and my mum's face as they were near to tears having to explain to me that I couldn't drive and why.

Again the frustration was immense and would usually be followed straight after by a spell of depression.

The problem was that the frustration was becoming more and more frequent and the spells of depression lasting longer and longer.

Soon after coming home, I'd bring up the same

3

argument – 'What do you mean I can't go down the boxing gym?'

I just couldn't understand it. I'd turn around to my mum and say, 'So what – I've had an operation. Why can't I fight? That's all I know. I've been fighting all me life mam.'

She'd reply, 'You've got a piece of skull missing from your head Paul, you can't.'

I just wouldn't accept it. She must have got sick of hearing me go on, 'I just want that rematch against Naz, mam. Win, lose or draw, that's the last fight I promise.'

I can only imagine how heartbreaking it must have been for my mum to continually listen to.

Despite the fact I could see her getting emotional, she never broke down in front of me although I imagine she probably shed many tears in private.

As if that wasn't enough, I had developed really bad mood swings. One minute I'd be laughing with everyone and saying, 'Let's go into town for a drink.' I'd limp over to the door in my dressing gown and then realise it was shut.

I'd turn around to my mum and ask, 'Who's got the keys? Why is the door locked? This is like a prison.'

Quietly, she'd reply, 'You can't go out yet Paul. You're not ready' and I'd break out into tears. The fact is, it had been done for my own safety. If I had wondered off into town completely disorientated, I could have easily walked in front of a car or decided to go for a swim in the sea.

I was never physically violent to anyone but verbally I'd become very aggressive and it was purely down to frustration.

I was like a kid again but the worst part was, although I didn't understand why I was in this condition, I was very aware that I was far less able than I had been at an earlier point in my life.

When it got to the point I couldn't cope, instead of shouting and screaming anymore, I'd just go silent and not speak to anyone.

It was the only way I could deal with it. In the end, I'd usually just fall asleep on the sofa.

I went to counselling for five weeks after I got home but I'm a pretty good actor and convinced them I was happy and looking forward to getting on with the rest of my life.

I was never suicidal, but I was certainly very depressed. As time ticked on, I lost interest in any hobbies such as playing snooker with my mates and when it came to exercise, something that was so natural to me, more and more I'd tell my mum, 'What's the point?'

'Scarborough has been rescued time and time again – sometimes by outsiders for their own purposes and profit, but more often by its own inhabitants. Repeatedly, their energy, civic pride and determined persistence have reformed and revitalised a community that appeared doomed to stagnation and irreversible decline.'

- Jack Binns,
History of Scarborough, *2003*

Round 2

□

Edgehill Estate

SCARBOROUGH has a number of famous dates etched in its history including being burnt down in 1066 and having the title of 'Britain's first seaside resort', bestowed upon it in the 1600s. On the 22nd June, 1972 I added to its timeline. I had no intention of being famous, I was just another kid off the Edgehill estate who was very proud of where he came from and, as luck would have it, blessed with a half decent left hook.

I was born at Scarborough Hospital, which was handy for my mum in terms of getting an ambulance as it was just down the road. For two days I was just known by everybody who came to see me as 'Baby Ingle,' or 'Greedy Ingle' as the nurses named me, because of the amount I was eating. The staff there couldn't believe how strong I was and the size of my hands for a new born. Within my first two days I'd managed to move myself to the top of the crib without any help from anybody. I guess I was bored and wanted to get home. That would become a common theme for me in later life.

The Yorkshire Hunter

Two days old, my mum named me Paul Andrew Ingle. There were about four Paul Ingle's in Scarborough already but she decided that was the name I would go by. She had a brother called Andrew but also nine other siblings, so my name could have been a lot longer. She chose Andrew for no other reason than she liked the name, although the irony would be that he was the one who got me interested in boxing a few years later.

We grew up with my grandad, mum's father, at the family house. My grandmother passed away a couple of years before I was born. By the time I arrived, mum had two jobs on the estate – one at the post office come grocery shop and the other in the community centre crèche. Whilst still cooking and cleaning for me and her nine other siblings, she never complained once. Our family were very supportive of her. If she was ever short or needed to borrow anything, they would always help out and if she needed someone to look after me they always obliged.

By the age of three, we had a newcomer to the family, my brother Dean. As kids, we got on really well. As brothers do, we would inevitably have some scraps, but as brothers we grew very close.

Around the same time as Dean's arrival, I started to attend nursery at Hinderwell Primary, followed by junior school the year after. As opposed to many kids, I loved every minute of school at that point – I stress, at that point! I found all the subjects interesting but particularly enjoyed getting stuck into art, woodwork, pottery and anything practical. However, from a young age, sport was the big passion for me.

I never got to know my dad as he scarpered when I was very young. In all honesty, I've never had any interest to look for him and couldn't really care less where he is or what's happened to him. My mum is number one to me and my brother and is worth a hundred of him. Nobody could have raised me the way she did. Nobody.

****

I PICKED up my first nickname at the age of seven. Going to the barbers was a luxury as a kid, so my grandad used to cut mine and Dean's hair in the kitchen. He would sit us on a chair with a towel around our neck and then get cracking with the scissors.

On this particular occasion, my mum walked in and had a look of horror and laughter on her face all at once. She was in tears before turning to grandad and saying, 'What have you done?' He's got patches all over his head. He looks like a leopard.' It was a mess. My mum dragged me to Steven's on Seamer Road to sort it out but the proposed solution wasn't great.

Within a matter of seconds of seeing it, he turned to my mum and said, 'Carol – the only way I can even it is by making his hair short. Very short.' She replied, 'Do what you need to.' This was 1979, a time when long hair was the fashion and short was associated with hooligans.

The next day I went to school with a big, thick cotton bobble hat on. But it was June and roasting hot. All my mates kept asking me why I wouldn't take the hat off but I refused and after a while started crying. One of the teachers then came over and made me.

The second I pulled the hat off, all my mates started chanting, 'Skinhead, skinhead', but I knew they were just messing about and within seconds I started laughing with them. The teacher wasn't angry, she was just concerned I was crying, but when she saw me laughing with my mates, she left me to it.

The Yorkshire Hunter

That was the birth of 'skin.' To this day, my mates I grew up with still call me that and since that haircut I've never grown my hair long again!

****

AS with pretty much everything in my life during the early years, the school I attended was on my estate which meant that most of my mates I grew up with also attended Hinderwell, which was a real bonus. Wayne Smith, Kenny Brocklehurst, Daz Smith and many others became like family to me. We were always in and out of each other's houses all the time, but I'm guessing Wayne must have liked our house a hell of a lot because he now lives in that very same place.

I have good memories of that house we grew up in. It was very fashionably decked out – for back then anyway. Multi-coloured stone effect lino flooring throughout with some quality wood style wallpaper around the fireplace and, to finish it all off, woodchip wallpaper on every wall, painted such a bright orange you almost didn't need to turn the lights on. The only bit of added colour I would have loved at that time was on the television. That said, many families didn't have one at all so we were very grateful to have our black and white 12 incher even if the reception was snowy.

My grandad was the governor of that domain. He had his specific chair in the lounge which is where you could find him most of the time, either reading the paper or watching the television. However, when he fell asleep, that's when I'd take control.

Even at the age of seven, I used to love my electronic games but played them so much that I'd always run out of batteries. The second he fell asleep I'd take out the ones from his hearing aid so I could keep on playing. Once I'd knackered them out, I'd pop them back in and nobody was any the wiser.

When he then turned it on the day after, he'd complain to my mum, 'I think me hearing aid has packed in again, Carol. I only put new batteries in yesterday, so it's definitely faulty.' He never did find out so, grandad, if you're looking down on me, 'Sorry!'

****

A YEAR later, we moved out of my grandad's house and to Lismore Road, which was still on the Edgehill estate, and were there for next 18 years. Mum was starting to spend more and more time with her dad as he'd suffered a stroke and needed looking after.

On the school front, my creative talents were blossoming by the week as I took to the stage and the lead role in the school musical at Hinderwell Primary. My mum had no idea what I would come out looking like, she was just there as the proud parent supporting her son. I don't remember what the play was called, but as the curtain went back and the music started, I came out singing and dancing to 'We are the Israelites', bouncing around the stage in a white T-shirt, a black leather jacket and a pair of Doc Marten boots looking like a proper 1970s skinhead. When I did have the chance to look over at my mum she was laughing so hard she nearly fell off her chair. So much for my moment of fame. I think there's a video still floating around somewhere, but it certainly won't be going on YouTube if I've got anything to do with it.

Out of school, my interest in bikes, both pedal and motor was becoming a big part of my life. So much so that many of my friends and family genuinely believed I might even go down that route as a career.

The Yorkshire Hunter

I had my first bike when I was two years old and because my legs weren't long enough, my grandad built wooden blocks onto the pedals so I could reach them. With them in place I was off. All I wanted for Christmas from then on was a new bike each year. And that's exactly what I got, I was very lucky.

As much as I loved my own bike, there was always one I wanted to ride which was not mine. My uncle Pete used to have this really nice racer in his shed and although I didn't officially have permission from him, I kind of assumed he'd be ok with me 'borrowing' it from time to time, especially as I knew the secret place where he hid the shed key.

Uncle Pete's was a proper adult racing bike that could clock up serious speed. The only problem was, again, that I could hardly reach the pedals. I used to have to lean it to one side to get on and then sit on the bar in the middle to keep it going. Once I'd managed to get it moving, I loved it, although it must have looked odd to see an eight year old on it as I passed by.

I thought I was taking part in a Grand Prix and, on one occasion, flew through the estate making loud motorcycle noises before realising that the person I'd swerved round on the pavement was uncle Pete. Thankfully, he saw the funny side of it and still winds me up about what I sounded like.

Our neighbours and good friends, the Amos family were a big influence on the bike front. I'd constantly be hanging out with John's daughters Dawn, Ali and Caroline, but it was his workshop at the back of their garden that I had a real fascination with from a very young age. John was a bit of a Jack of all trades and would always have stuff like washing machines lying around that he'd be repairing.

He knew I loved my bikes and would often repair

mine whenever it went bust – which was quite often. He'd never make a fuss and, if he saw me struggling, he'd always help out. Whenever I was at their house, his wife would spoil me rotten with pop and ice cream. A truly lovely family.

There was also a guy across the road called Mr Welford who used to fix bikes for free in his shed. He just loved doing it and could make a bike from the scrap left behind from others; one big wheel, a little one, flash handlebars, whatever was going he could fashion it into something.

Between Mr Welford and John Amos it was almost like I'd had an apprenticeship and I felt pretty confident stripping bikes down and rebuilding them exactly how I wanted.

On one particular day, I went round to John's workshop and saw him and a couple of his mates working on this big metal cylinder. When they plugged it in and started it up, it made this loud roaring noise. I had never seen anything like it before and, with all three of them working on it, assumed it was very important. Being an inquisitive lad, I asked him what it was and John replied with a serious face, 'It's a spaceship Paul and we are looking for a pilot.' I couldn't believe it, a spaceship, here, on the Edgehill estate!

I told John straight away, 'I can fly one of them' and he replied back, cautiously, 'Have you had any lessons?' Obviously I told him I had and, at that moment, decided that I wanted to be the first kid in the world to travel to outer space. I even measured myself alongside the cylinder to check I'd fit inside and was pencilling where the window could be built in.

I ran straight home and told my mum that I was going to the moon and asked if she had a spare crash helmet and some goggles. She looked at me a little surprised and said, 'I'll see what I can find Paul.'

The Yorkshire Hunter

The next day, John had me going through some landing jump drills and also told me that the following morning I would need to practise with the correct clothing because it would be freezing in outer space. So, I turned up wearing a leather jacket, two jumpers and borrowed a pair of heavy boots. A mate of mine had even lent me a backpack for my rations on board.

This went on for weeks. Every day John would set me a new task and every day I would complete it, eager to learn everything about becoming Edgehill's first ever space cadet. After a few weeks John came out and told me it was all a wind up and the spaceship was actually a water heater.

Apparently his wife told him to stop leading me on and that was that. They kept reminding me of the joke well in to my teenage years and, ironically, I now hate flying.

With the amount I started to cycle, I quickly became an expert on dealing with punctures. Me and my mates used to tackle any terrain on our bikes, whether they were built for it or not. I'd have two or three punctures a day sometimes and could have easily been one of the guys who worked in the Formula One pit lanes such was my speed and prowess in fixing them.

The Amos family were massive motorbike racing fans and at one point were even sponsoring one of the Moto GP bikes at Cadwell Park. At least once a year, they would organise for a big group to go down to see the races and, knowing how much I loved it, John would pile me with his family into their big van and we'd make a weekend of it. It was one of the highlights of my year.

At the time, Barry Sheen was the world champion and everyone idolised him, including me. Once, I perched on my uncle Pete's shoulders at Cadwell Park so I could get a good view of Barry in the paddock. I immediately turned round and said, 'Uncle Pete, I'm gonna be famous one day. I'm gonna be a world champion.' He wasn't convinced.

On one of the trips there, I went missing among the thousands there and started to cause a real concern, especially with the Lincolnshire circuit being among woodland. Everyone I'd travelled there with was frantically looking for me.

A couple of hours earlier, I'd been walking past this big zipped up tent with John Amos when I spotted Barry Sheen through one of the gaps. I couldn't believe it. I turned to John excitedly and said, 'It's Barry Sheen! I'm going to get in there and meet him.' John responded, 'You can't just walk in there. We'll need to ask permission.' But I thought to myself, without letting on to anybody that I'd find a way.

I went back to the spot, on my own, a couple of hours later, squeezed through the gap and walked straight into the tent. Barry took a look and I'm not sure if he initially felt sorry for me because I was just a tiny little lad, but he soon realised I'd a real passion for his bike and knew everything about him.

Instead of booting me out, he told his crew to let me stay as long as I wanted and never once made me feel like I needed to leave. In fact he had me running about the different paddocks doing stuff for him, picking up papers, bottles of water and food, most of which I ended up eating myself. I was loving it.

In the meantime, whilst desperately trying to find me, John Amos spotted me from a distance and shouted but with a smile on his face and waving a clenched fist in the air. By this stage I was sitting on Barry Sheen's bike asking him about what every button and lever did and how fast it could go in a straight line, round bends and even whether he could take me for a spin on it.

Despite the fact that there was a line of people waiting

outside to have their photo taken with him or get an autograph, Barry and his pit crew were fantastic in answering all my questions. With the exception of not taking me for that spin around the track, it was a wonderful afternoon.

I was so inspired by the whole experience I did seriously think about becoming a biker and managed to live the dream for a few months courtesy of John Amos's moped which he lent me. I used to drive it flat out around the fields at the back of the estate with the other gangs of lads, with my head down and legs tucked in tight to the frame, thinking I was on the last lap of a big race at Cadwell. In the end it blew up and I was in tears. Maybe it was for the best though, as I was only eight and didn't have a license.

I did manage to pay John back though but perhaps not in a way he expected. A few months later, we were at Donington Park watching the motorbikes and we walked past a big industrial catering truck on the way to John's van to have some lunch. I asked what was in the truck and John jokingly said, 'That's a kitchen. Take a look and see if they have anything for us.'

I ran over and managed to get inside the window and there were trays of steaks piled up. With nobody in sight, I found a few carrier bags and started pulling out one after the other and went over to John with a big grin on my face and couple of big bags full of meat. I don't think he was that delighted but he wasn't going to take them back in case I got in any trouble. On the upside, he was eating steak for about a month.

****

I LOVED my time at Hinderwell Primary but, at the age of 11, it was time to move on to Graham (senior secondary)

School. Although the likes of Wayne and a few of my other mates were also coming with me, in all honesty, I didn't enjoy my time there one bit. The teachers were too strict and, in my mind, I'd already decided that all I wanted to do was pursue a certain sport.

I had already lost interest in subjects like maths and history and just wanted to be in the gym. Although I'm now able to understand why I needed education, at the time I just thought the school was being difficult.

My mum was a great help in terms of keeping me focused with school but unfortunately there was only so much she could do. I used to bring back homework all the time and my mum would say, 'Make sure you do it before training, Paul.' I'd always shout back. 'I'll do it when I come back,' but I never did.

As a result, I started getting lots of detention. I realised after a while that serving them was taking up valuable training time, so in the end I buckled down a little bit and showed my face at school enough to keep the teachers happy. It all worked out in the end because the school became proud of my sporting achievements but I knew from an early age I wasn't an academic.

****

AS I approached my teenage years, I couldn't have asked for more living in Scarborough. I had the seafront, loads of open spaces to explore with my mates, fishing down the Mere pond and the non-stop drama on the estate I lived on.

We were always out to impress the girls on a Saturday down the roller disco. Everybody from Edgehill was there, so looking cool was always high on the agenda for us. Whilst everybody else was doing laps wearing helmets, knee and elbow pads, me and Wayne Smith would cruise around with our flat caps on. Cool first – safety second. We'd often come home covered in cuts and bruises, but somehow, throughout my life I've never broken a bone.

I also had my first form of pocket money around that time, although it wasn't from my mum. Down on the seafront arcades, we would go 'machine banging'. These were the days before they started to alarm them so we'd casually walk past and give them a good smack and sometimes a few coins would drop. With about 20 or 30 pennies in our pockets we felt like we'd struck it rich and would treat ourselves to some chips or sweets. Most times we'd walk out without anybody noticing, but on others the security guards would clock us and give chase, although they never managed to catch us.

I always thought I could get past my mum, but the second I walked through the door with my pockets jingling full of coins, she noticed straight away – her radar for sound was incredible, but her bullshit detector was even better. She would say, 'Where did you get that cash?' I'd tell her I won it on the one-armed bandits but she knew I was lying. I soon developed some great bobbing and weaving skills.

Probably the only thing I did manage to pull the wool over my mum's eyes for, over many years, was skiving off school. It was only revealed a few years ago when my mum was reminiscing with her sister, my auntie Jen, about me as a kid and she suddenly turned to me and said, 'I bet you never told your mam about when you used to skive school when you were about 13 did you?' That was it, the cat was out of the bag.

I had my routine down to a tee. I'd leave my house then wait at the stop until the bus was close to arriving before diving into the hedge and waiting for it to pull away. After a couple of minutes, I'd check the coast was clear and that my mum or any of my neighbours or family hadn't spotted me,

and I'd go and see my auntie Jen and ask her if she could tell
the school that I felt poorly. She knew I was skiving and even
used to write me sick notes on behalf of my mum if I needed
them. She was first class.

My uncle Pete also used to help us out. One day, I was
walking down the Valley towards the beach, when he spotted
me. I ran over to him and pleaded, 'Please don't tell me
mam!' His main concern was not her but my welfare. He was
more worried that I didn't get into any mischief or go hungry,
so he gave me a couple of quid to get some food and told me,
'Don't forget to get home at the right time, as if you were
leaving school.' Said like a pro.

The funny thing is that those who covered for me
thought they were the only ones doing it and kept deadly
quiet about it. It's only now, whilst writing this book, that we
are all able to look back and laugh. For any kids reading this,
as they say on all the programmes, 'Don't do this at home'.
Always get yourself an education to fall back on.

Unfortunately, I started to influence my brother with
my ways. By this time, I had a number of routines up my
sleeve. For one, as we were waiting for the bus, I'd hold him
back and say, 'Stand here and let it set off.' He asked why and
I explained to him, 'As the bus leaves from the stop, we'll
sprint after it shouting, "Wait for us!"' Obviously, it was
hardly sprinting, more like *Chariots of Fire* in slow motion but
in that way, Irene who ran the shop across the road would
clearly see and hear us.

Straight afterwards, we would go home and continue
with our Oscar-winning performance, by telling mum what
had happened and asking her to double-check with Irene
who'd seen it all. Later, when mum used to go up there to
collect the evening paper, Irene would confirm our hard luck
story.

****

I DIDN'T miss not having holidays as a kid because I never really had any. Apart from a trip to Germany with my auntie Margy and her family when I was about 12 and a day trip with mum and my brother to Butlins, I never went away until I was in my late teens, with my mates.

Money was tight and I knew mum did everything she could to make ends meet and gave us all she could, regardless. We did like most families on the estate and were perfectly happy with anything that came our way, so we become creative with what was on our doorstep.

Swimming in the Scarborough Mere pond or fishing for newts at the local disused clay quarry were perhaps not the safest options for kids, but they provided us with adventures.

The Edgehill estate was notoriously tough. It was one of the smaller ones in Scarborough and despite having earned the title 'cardboard city', due to the number of broken windows covered up with broken-down boxes, everybody knew each other and most of the time we never locked our front doors. We had no reason to.

Although the estate was full of crooks, they were very loyal. They looked after us in fact. If there were any strangers walking around, they would ask them what they were doing on our patch. As I started to progress with my sports, those on the Edgehill estate remained very loyal to me. I knew no better – it was always home to me and I had nothing else to compare it with. However, for an incomer, I can see how it would have looked pretty intimidating.

A couple of times every week, cars would be broken into or stolen from the local area and lads as young as 12 would drag race them down the estate road. One time they were speeding down the road at such a rate that they lost control and crashed metres away from our house. The lads just got out the car and did a runner all laughing at the buzz of what they had just done. By the morning, the car had been set on fire which just added to the collection of other vehicles and motorbikes that had been torched. We got on with our lives and just dealt with it.

Whilst getting my book together I only recently found out the full details of a story which made me realise that my fighting spirit certainly comes from my mum. It takes a lot to push her to breaking point but one morning, around four o'clock, a group of lads were creating so much noise and disruption that it was keeping us all up. I heard my mum shout, 'I'm not having this,' and she walked out of the front door. Apparently, as a car was coming down Lismore Road like a race track, she picked up a brick and hurled it straight through one of its windows at about 50 miles an hour. They got the message.

Drugs and alcohol abuse were a big concern on the estate at the time. It was mainly people sniffing stuff from plastic bags or using needles. When my mum worked at the crèche in the community centre, the first job she always had to do was clear up all the mess from the 'bag sniffers' and druggies before the kids were dropped off.

The drinking problem for some was so bad that on a number of occasions I witnessed a certain father and son beating each other up on their way back from the social club. Sadly both have passed away, one died from cancer and the other from the effects of alcohol. Very sad.

With all this going on, my mum made sure that me and my brother certainly didn't mess about. Her method of discipline was old school yet very effective. If we messed about she would bring out the slipper. One night, when I was about 13, my mum let my mates camp in the garden and she came out to us at 10pm and said, 'Lights out,' and then she went back upstairs to bed. At about midnight we snuck off to the playground and started playing on the swings. Mum heard us laughing and making a racket and she came flying down. She told my friends to go home and me to get upstairs. That's when the slipper came off. Every step I took upstairs I got a smack. I never forget that there were 17 on that staircase. Then my mum gave me a few more when I got to bed to round it up to 20.

Mum only tapped us. She was great and just wanted to make sure we grew up with discipline in our lives. You would sometimes hear horrifying stories about little kids banging on their parents doors at midnight because they'd been locked out for, maybe, asking to go to the toilet or wanting a glass of water and then couldn't get back in because their parents had passed out from sinking numerous cans of lager or overdosed on heroin.

Many of the people on the estates lived to sad extremes because they were unemployed or had left school at 11 and were terminally bored. When you are in that situation, you tend to look for things to keep you occupied. It wasn't uncommon to see heroin addicts as young as 12 or 13, excessive gamblers or alcoholics a little older and teenage pregnancies were also very common.

When money ran out for many people, they would join one of the gangs to feel safety in numbers, so that they could get cash for their habits. It was a slippery slope which many were never able to climb back from and, unfortunately, most of the gang activities on the estates either led to a life of crime or death.

Compared to some of the families on the estate, me

and my brother were very lucky to have such an incredible parent. We are all products of our own environment and she was a great role model of how to live and make the best. There wasn't a great science behind her method either – she simply taught us the difference between right and wrong.

She managed to raise us on next to nothing but never made it an issue. What she never did was cut corners and that rubbed off on me. Although she may not have agreed with the crappy benefits the government were giving back in those days, she never took matters into her own hands to make ends meet illegally.

And, if we ever came off the rails, it was never from anything our mum taught us. In fact, discipline from her and a few other people turned out to be key in my life from a very young age.

'**K**eep an eye on him, he's
a good boy. He's going
to go a long way.'
- Paddy Govier, circa 1980 -
Paul Ingle's first boxing coach

Round 3
□
Putting on the Gloves

AS a young lad I think I tried every sport available in Scarborough. I really liked rugby but as I grew older I became cheesed off because I was so small compared to the other lads. I had fun and success with table tennis, football, snooker and even roller skating, but there was one sport which had a spell over me, even when I didn't fancy going.

Although my grandad had boxed in the army and was a father figure and disciplinarian to me growing up, he never forced boxing on me. Whichever sport I took up and in fact whatever I showed an interest in, he encouraged me and supported me in any way he could.

The person who initially got me interested in boxing was my uncle Andrew – or 'Tubby' as he's known to the locals. He was only 10 years older than me, so was almost like an older brother, someone I looked up to.

His route into boxing was pretty simple. He used to go to school with a lad called Mike Simpson who was the son of local boxing coach Ray Simpson. One day Mike said to Andrew, 'I notice you hang around on the street corners a lot.

The Yorkshire Hunter

There are too many bad distractions out there for you. Why don't you come up to the boxing club with me? It's only five minutes from the estate?' And that was that. Andrew had 17 amateur fights in his mid-teens, of which he won 11, but carried on training for a number of years afterwards.

Around the age of seven, I started going down to the boxing gym. It used to be a community centre for kids in the early days but, with the exception of the occasional disco, it was never that busy. Then the boxing kind of took over the place and it's still going strong today.

For those first few visits we never actually went inside, just stared through the windows as I was worried my uncle might see me and I didn't want to distract him. I was mesmerised by the routines he was doing on the speed ball, the heavy bag and on the pads with the trainers, but it was always the last part which got my hair standing on end – when he stepped through the ropes to spar.

After a few weeks I became more and more curious and plucked up the courage to pop my head around the gym door. My uncle Andrew had seen me and said, 'You keep looking through the window, why don't you just come up with me next time?' That turned out to be the first day of the rest of my life.

As with many activities I did as a kid, a bunch of us started at the same time. Wayne Smith, Peter Davis, Paul Barnett, Daz Smith, myself and a few others all got stuck in three nights a week. However, over time, most of them either got bored or decided it just wasn't for them.

I, on the other hand, loved it from the moment I stepped into the gym. Ok, well, maybe not straight away. Uncle Andrew started putting me in the ring with other kids and would pop the gloves on and say, 'There you go Paul. Have a little spar.'

When I got hit I used to take them off and throw them on the canvas and start to cry. At first, I used to come home crying to my mum wailing, 'I'm not going up there again. They're beating me up.' But I did used to go back. Again and again.

After a few months, I soon realised that I didn't want to 'play' at boxing. Some of the lads who took part used to cut corners in training or stop when the trainers weren't looking, but I did the full lot. In fact I wanted more than that at first. The atmosphere and the buzz of the gym was like a magnet.

I used to love watching the bigger guys mastering their routines and wanted to be able to do them with the same level of precision. When I first started skipping I was tripping up and couldn't get the rhythm straight away.

I'd see the others working it at great speed, only coming about a centimetre off the ground, moving the rope around them and side to side so fast you could barely see it, just hear the rope whizzing through the air. The same went with the pads. I'd see some of the top lads doing five, seven or 10 punch combinations in a flash, just at the command of the trainer. But when I tried it for the first time I was throwing all kinds of punches because I couldn't remember the order or wasn't sure of the correct names.

Even at the age of seven, it didn't take me long to realise that boxing was a sport that required a great deal of intelligence, which is probably the last thing most people would think, unless you've stepped into the ring.

In order for me to hit and not to get hit, I realised that I needed to get the right people around me to develop my boxing brain. I needed guidance on timing, footwork, movement, angles and stamina training. Most of the terms I didn't even really understand as a little kid – but I was very eager to learn. The three men who initially helped me, turned out to be a lifelong influence on my journey ahead.

****

PAT GOVIER, or Paddy as he was known to everyone at the boxing club, lived an incredible life and positively influenced so many people he came into contact with, especially me. He was like the old man in the *Rocky* films. He quickly saw that I had potential and made me believe in myself.

Born in 1908 and standing around five feet tall, he came from the East End of London which is where he first started boxing. When he was in the army he married a woman from Scarborough and then took a leap of faith and moved up here to start and raise his family. I'm so glad he did.

He used to tell us stories about how he attempted to get food on the table during the Great Depression of the 1930s when everybody was struggling to survive, never mind make ends meet. Back then, boxing matches would be organised in Scarborough between people who were unemployed or staying at the YMCA, with groceries being the prize. He recounted, 'I wanted those groceries so badly because my family was hungry and so was I.'

He learned the need to be elusive and fit. Paddy used to say that he wanted to win every fight but he also needed to make sure that he didn't take a lot of punches so that he could compete the next week.

If he came back covered in lumps, bumps and bruises, they wouldn't allow him to go again and that would mean no food on the table. That thought stayed with me throughout my career.

Paddy was proper old school with his training

techniques. Having fought over 100 fights as an amateur – winning nearly all of them – and then turning pro in the late 1920s, he picked up some great methods along the way.

He'd show me old photos of what he used to look like and for someone who had been through so much, to pass on his boxing knowledge to me so passionately was massive.

He had this primitive catapult-style device which was basically a ball on the end of a long piece of elastic and he would flick it at my face at different angles when I was in range. The purpose was to get me to slip and move my head. Truth be told, he had a good aim and hit me quite a few times.

As a little kid who had just started boxing I used to come back home to my mum crying, 'Paddy hit me on the nose with the ball.' She'd say, 'Don't be so daft. You're gonna get worse than that in the future, so go back tomorrow and learn some more.'

Most of my mates had already decided that getting punched in the face wasn't for them and started to attend less and less, but I kept on coming back for some reason. In the early days, I'd be the same scratched record to my mum when walking through the doors, 'I'm not going back there. They're mean and bully me.'

Over time I realised that the pain I was complaining about wasn't actually that bad. Half of the reason I was crying was because of the fear of the unknown. I was so worried about what it would be like to get hit in the eye or the nose that when it happened, I was a wreck.

The first time I got hit with a punch in the stomach I fell to the floor and was winded so badly I couldn't speak.

Paddy would tell me, 'Paul, there's not a boxer on this planet who at some point in their early days didn't cry or get hurt and thought about never coming back. The strength in character comes when you jump back into that ring knowing it could happen again. That's how all champions start.'

I became far quicker and better equipped with my defence so that I didn't take the full brunt of a punch. Paddy used to chant a mantra in the gym, 'If they can't hit you, they can't hurt you. And if they can't hurt you, they can't beat you.' I took it on board.

My confidence rocketed within a short space of time. At the end of a sparring session, they would match two kids up and it was always my hand which was first up in the air. Many others would wait just to make sure they wouldn't be in against somebody tougher than them. Eight years old and I wasn't worried about how big, strong or aggressive the other kid was – I just wanted to be in there.

****

BY that time, I distinctly remember the other kids at the boxing club getting really frustrated with me. The truth is I wasn't even making a conscious decision to get out of the way of punches, it had just become natural – as natural as breathing.

After mastering my head movement, we then concentrated on the rest of my armoury. Paddy noted that my speed, balance and accuracy was unbelievable for my age and added, 'If you hit your opponent on the right spot, they will go down.' Bit by bit it was all making more sense.

Now, two other trainers also became a major part of my coaching especially as Paddy was starting to get on in years and his health was worsening. Like Paddy, Tommy Johnson and Ray Simpson were absolute gentlemen. Tommy was the lead trainer with Ray as the assistant coach. Funnily enough, Tommy was also trained by Paddy when he was a young lad.

I always remember Paddy saying to Tommy in front of me, 'Keep an eye on him, he's a good boy. He's going to go a long way.' I've forgotten a few things over the years, but that comment has stuck with me my whole life.

The club meant a great deal to the three of them and was more than just a place to train. In the early days, Scarborough Amateur Boxing Club didn't have the facilities that many other clubs did and, on occasions, didn't even have a hall to train in.

Ray was friendly with a guy called Billy Hall who was a legendary trainer in Hull who would often give our club some free equipment because he knew we were very short. We were very grateful for any support but without proper equipment and facilities, we simply improvised and made do with whatever was on offer. The boxing club was a place run and used by passionate people. They made it, and it didn't matter if we were training in a field or in a ring made from four chairs.

In those days, most of the lads at Scarborough ABC were from the Edgehill estate, many of whom had fiery characters. The one thing we learned very quickly was discipline, basically because Tommy didn't tolerate anybody messing about in his place.

I can still see him going into the changing rooms after everybody had got changed and inspecting. If Tommy saw that the kids hadn't folded their clothes up correctly in their bag he'd say, 'Look, your parents paid good money for these. Fold 'em properly and be respectful.' The lads listened to everything he said and we did as he asked. We didn't realise it at the time but we were also starting to get our first few lessons in life training too.

My mum didn't get me into boxing so I could defend myself but I know that she was glad I learned to take care of myself. None of the other kids used to mess around with me but I never started with them either. In fact, I never had a single fight on the Edgehill estate. It was all done in the ring and I'm glad it continued that way throughout my life.

****

IT was Tommy who first spotted my 'southpaw crisis'. When I was sparring, I did so out of an orthodox stance but pretty much everything I threw was off my left hand. My right stayed glued to my jaw.

That's when Tommy picked up on something nobody else had seen up to that point.

He asked, 'Do you write with your right hand, lad?'

I said, 'No, I write with me left.'

He advised, 'In that case, put your right foot forward because you're a southpaw.'

I replied, 'But I feel comfortable with my left in front.'

He didn't care. 'I don't like southpaws either, Paul' he told me. 'I'd shoot them at birth if I had my way. They are awkward buggers to train and fight. But you are naturally left-handed, so you need to lead with your right.'

I wasn't happy.

I felt like everything was back to front and very unnatural so I kept changing back to orthodox. Tommy would go mad and start shouting, 'What are you doing? Change back, you are a southpaw Paul, you box with your strong hand at the back'.

I would do that for, maybe, another 10 seconds and without thinking bounced straight back to what felt more comfortable.

This went on for about a month until, one day, Tommy said, 'Paul, don't you like southpaw?'

I replied, 'I can't do it properly Tommy'.

He then said, 'But you're going to have no power in your right hand. It's going to be all about your left.'

I told him, 'That's fine, I'll box with me left then'.

He replied, 'But you need two hands in boxing'.

We stopped, looked at each other and laughed.

After a few weeks he could see I was getting good results as an unnatural orthodox fighter and said, 'Just stay as you are Paul. I think you'll be just fine'.

****

BY the age of 11, I was ready for my first official test. Or so I thought. My first club fight show was held at the Corner Café on Scarborough seafront, as part of a boxing dinner sponsored by the local Lions Club.

I was up second on the bill but I was so nervous I spent most of the time beforehand on the toilet. I remember sitting on the loo and Tommy coming into the changing rooms and checking on me.

'Everything alright, Paul?'

I replied, 'I've been to the toilet a few times.'

He said, 'Don't worry, that's because your adrenaline is working well.' I had absolutely no idea what that was. I even recall looking down at the toilet thinking, 'Is that what adrenaline looks like?'

After overcoming my fears, I put on my boxing vest and popped my hands straight into the boxing gloves as no hand wraps were needed back in those days for kids – or headguards come to think of it.

I walked out to a tightly packed full house with a great reception from the people who had come to support their local five-stone seven-pounder.

The parents of the fighters always stood at the back because it was a proper dinner function. My mum was with friends and family and although she made out to be quite calm, she was a bag of nerves. If she'd been allowed to smoke a fag in the hall, she would have. There was a friend of hers who was so nervous for me that she was crying as I was coming out.

With the ring in sight, my nerves hit their peak but I tried to act brave and unfazed by everything and continued to walk forward. Tommy was trying to calm me down and said, 'Come on Paul, you'll be fine when you get in there.' It was appreciated but didn't help.

As we stepped through the ropes Tommy said, 'I want to see fast hands, keep that head down and fire off those straight punches. You'll be too strong for him.' I was really pumped up but the nerves didn't disappear during the fight. At the end of each round I vomited on a number of occasions, well actually it was more gagging, there was nothing left in my stomach.

Although my opponent was a bit taller than me, I beat him up for all three of the one-and-a-half minute rounds doing exactly what Tommy told me. Soon after the final bell, I was presented with a trophy that was almost as big and heavy as me, which thankfully Tommy carried back to the changing room.

With my first win under my belt, I felt like a world champion. I looked over and saw my mum clapping and cheering – again, another great memory. Mind you, the second I started making my way back to the changing room I saw her sprinting outside for a fag to calm herself down.

When we got back to the changing room, I asked Tommy, 'When do I fight next?'

He was calm and with a grin on his face just said, 'You

need a few days rest Paul, then we'll get you in the ring again.' True to his word, he had me fighting within a week and then pretty much every week after that.

Starting off with such a great win meant nothing, I went on to lose my next four fights. Tommy never let me lose faith, though, and kept telling me to stick with it and have faith in my ability.

'**N**one of his punches as
an amateur or a pro
happened by accident.
Hard work, repetition and self-
belief made it work.'
- *Ray Simpson, Paul Ingle's
amateur boxing coach*

Round 4

□

Hooked on the Left Hook

BY the age of 12, I was starting to train and live the life of a boxer. I would get up around 6am, put my sweat gear on, which included a layer of bin liners, then run for about 45 minutes at a good pace, no matter if it was freezing cold, boiling hot or blowing a gale.

On my return I'd have a light breakfast, usually a couple of slices of toast and a cup of tea and then head off to Graham secondary school.

That diet was almost as tough as the training. As a kid, I was pretty chubby. Tommy and Ray were always going on about it, trying to help me understand that if I wanted to go far in the sport I needed to watch what I was eating.

They even tried to approach my mum about it but she told them, 'I'm not sure where he gets his money from but he's always at the chip shop.'

The problem was that in addition to my supper, Graham from the chippie used to give me and my mates free food. Pretty much every night he'd hand over fish, chips and peas and we would load it up with lashings of salt and vinegar.

In all honesty, I thought everybody was fussing over nothing. Then I had a day which made me think otherwise.

I was getting weighed in for a fight and topped the scales at four kilos over the limit. Although you were allowed two extra, I had to fight a lad in the division above as a result. He was taller and stronger than me and the second the fight was over I stormed out. I'd lost and I knew it was all down to me.

When we got back to the changing room, Ray asked me if I wanted to fight in the schoolboys championships knowing that it was my dream at that point. I told him that of course I did and he then set me a clever incentive.

'I'm not sure if you have the discipline because Christmas is coming up and the weigh-in for the schoolboys is directly afterwards,' he said. 'If you make that weight, you need to hold it for 10 weeks, the length of the schoolboy tournament. I just don't think you can do it.' They both knew I never backed down from a challenge.

****

IF I could have trained three times per day, seven days a week even at that stage I would have, but I was restricted to two hours on Monday, Wednesday and Friday evenings. I used to train in the kids session and then straight after I'd take part in the adults. Although I'd mix in some other sports such as football on a Thursday, my focus was all about the boxing. I had become obsessed with Paddy's mantra of hit and not get hit.

One evening, I was sparring with this kid and every time I hit him, he just couldn't land one back. He started to get angry and frustrated and then swinging haymakers. I thought to myself, 'I'm not having that' and went to work on him.

Tommy and Paddy had to jump in as things were getting out of hand. The other kid steamed out and Tommy told me to hit the bags instead. Five minutes later, the same kid rushed back in but with a rugby boot in his hand and started chasing me around the gym, wanting to smash it over my head.

Whilst my good mate Daz Smith was dying of laughter, I was running for my life. Thankfully Paddy and Tommy jumped in and that was the end of it although we didn't see that lad at the gym again.

I never used to go round telling anybody I boxed at school but I reckon the teachers started to guess after a while that I didn't get the black eyes and fat lips from playing table tennis. At first they were a little bit off with me but, over the years, they became very supportive and every time I won a competition they would bring me up on stage and announce my win, which was usually followed by a round of applause.

In fact, Mr Robinson, the Headmaster at the senior school came to see me box on a number of occasions. He was always very proud to see any of the lads from the Edgehill estate making something of themselves.

Originally from London, Lenny Cook was a really nice bloke and worked in my corner with Tommy on a number of occasions. However, he was also in charge of driving the boxing minibus and would always get lost. I could have understood it if he was unfamiliar with the area but Lenny was a long distance lorry driver.

To make it worse, on those long winter journeys, there was no heating inside the van and a big hole in the floor. We never successfully managed to close it, so it was absolutely perishing. Everybody would pile in wearing their caps, heavy jackets, gloves and scarves and then we would head off to the likes of Newcastle, Sunderland and Sheffield.

The Yorkshire Hunter

My mum, who followed me everywhere, would sit me on her knee to keep me warm and made sure I didn't go hungry or thirsty. She went above and beyond the call of duty for me.

John Amos was also very helpful when I was lacking transport in those early days, although he could be a little impatient. Once, as we pulled up to the boxing hall in his van with his family, he said to me, 'You're going to have to make this quick because we need to be home soon as I've got an early start tomorrow.'

I assured him that wouldn't be a problem and I'd be as quick as I could.

I was paired with this stocky lad and for the first 30 seconds was trying to suss him out. Next thing he threw a big right hand flush on my nose which not so much hurt me but made me mad.

Within a couple of seconds I knocked him down and the bout was called to a halt. I stuck my head through the ropes and said to John, 'Are you ready to go?' He was laughing and shaking his head at the same time and within 10 minutes we'd begun the journey back.

I owe a lot to John. He was a good neighbour, a great supporter of my boxing and a generous man.

When I first started competing, he told me, 'For every fight you win, I'll give you a pound.' With my grandad doing the same, I'd get up to £4 per week on some occasions. It was like being on wages.

****

AFTER about 30 amateur contests, I fought in the regional schoolboy tournament. I remember Ray asking me how I felt a couple of hours before the opening bout and I replied, 'I might not beat this kid today but I tell you what, I'll make sure he remembers me.'

I was representing Humberside & Yorkshire and had to get through the north east finals first, then the north west ones before getting to finals in Derby. I had eight fights in total, won them all and racked up my first valuable piece of silverware that would get me recognised in the boxing circles.

By this stage, I'm proud to say that I'd only been stopped once. I was fighting in Liverpool and this lad hit me a few times bang on the nose and blood was streaming down my face making a right mess. It wasn't broken but the ref decided to stop the fight.

My opponent was Alan Vaughan who later also boxed for England and turned out to be a good mate of mine. We ended up on the same medal-winning team in Peru and also travelled to the Olympics together. He was one of the best and most decorated amateur boxers I'd ever shared a ring with.

After our fight he apologised as he felt bad seeing all the blood. I, on the other hand, was fuming at the decision and took out my gumshield and threw it at the ref. I launched it so hard it went flying past him and Ray Simpson caught it in mid-air making out it had been a deliberate act.

Amateur boxing was great schooling not least because you could never be sure who you would be fighting next. There wasn't much chance to watch videos of your opponent or research their strengths and weaknesses, you just get in there and do the best you could. The strength I had at this stage was adaptability.

The year after, aged 13, I went on to win the 'Class A' schoolboys at York Hall in Bethnal Green. It was the first time I had been to London and was nervous on a number of fronts. Mum had organised a load of coaches to take us there and back and most of Edgehill and the surrounds came down to support me. Some of the areas we drove through in East London made me appreciate home, they were rough.

The guy I was fighting was much taller and was trying to take the piss out of me at the weigh-in, calling me names but I wasn't bothered with his games. I knew I had done my training and had a feeling that he was insulting me because he wasn't as confident.

When I walked out from the changing rooms both the lower and upper decks were packed. The support I had was immense and that was probably the first time I truly realised how loud my fans could be.

As the bell sounded for round one, my opponent tried taking my head off but I started ducking and weaving and then unleashed a right hand, followed by a left hook and put him down. They were probably the only two punches I threw in the fight but that was all that was needed.

The crowd went mad for the little lad from Scarborough who had stopped his bigger opponent in the first round. Everyone seemed to be clapping and shouting praise. I felt incredible. Tommy was nearly crying he was that proud. I did feel a bit sorry for my fans, though. We had all travelled about seven hours for a match that was over in about a minute.

By now, I was starting to clock up a serious amount of silverware. What started off as one trophy on a shelf turned into two, then a certificate, then a medal, then two shelves, followed by a cabinet, then two cabinets. Inside of three years of my amateur debut, we'd already started to run out of space and had to start putting most of the stuff into boxes and in the loft.

The only part I wasn't happy about was cleaning it all. Every couple of months or so mum would say, 'Don't make any plans this weekend, we're going to be cleaning your trophy cabinet.' I did it once and it took four hours and that was valuable time to go out on the bikes or hang out at the seafront.

Thankfully, in the early days, for some of the local competitions I was given the opportunity of choosing either a trophy or other prizes such as food, cutlery sets, suitcases, tools, televisions and so on.

I used to think about Paddy Govier and how he used to fight for food and it made me feel like a grittier fighter to accept groceries or household goods as a prize. Same went with the meals on offer for the junior boxers.

Most places I fought at I'd get a refreshment ticket which would usually be something like a couple of sandwiches, a pork pie and a drink. Very basic. If it was a posh club, you might get sausage and chips in a basket. I was always dead excited about what meal would be behind that ticket whereas the rich kids would turn their nose up at it and eat their packed lunches.

****

DURING the summer of 1986 I kept myself busy with my training but also tried my hand at a couple of jobs to earn a few quid. I took on a paper round and also worked at a café on the seafront, waiting tables in a fish and chip shop. In all honesty, I wasn't the best.

Although I had great balance in the ring, when you put a tray in my hands with two plates of fish and chips and a couple of mugs of tea on, I was a nightmare. I lost count how many I dropped in the first few weeks and was fed up of walking around with my head down and my face bright red, so I jacked that in pretty quick.

Around that time, my grandad passed away. With no dad around, he was a strict father figure to me and a very good friend. A distinguished looking man with jet black hair, a thin pencil-like moustache and roughly five feet five inches tall, he was loved by everyone in the community.

'Gentleman George' was an ex-army man who had worked and socialised in the local community all his life and was always there to help his close friends and family whenever they needed. Whether it was playing in the darts league or making sure his nearest never went short, he gave his all. George Ingle was given a good send off and the turnout at the funeral was massive.

Thankfully, boxing kept my mind busy and didn't let me get too down about my grandad. By the time I turned 14, Ray and Tommy were still working with me but Ray was starting to deal with more of my day-to-day coaching such as technique work and fitness training.

Tommy already had me hitting the medicine ball with my left hook but Ray pushed it to the next level. He could see that my hook was good but he wanted to make it sharper and stronger yet, at the same time, throw it at such speed that my opponent wouldn't be able to cover up.

Ray decided that as I was a southpaw firing out of an orthodox stance, who pretty much never threw a right hand, instead of it being a hindrance, he played it to my advantage. He used to tell me, 'Most of the guys you fight will see you in an orthodox stance, assume your left hand is the weak one and will be happy to stand in front of it. I want to push your left hand from being good, to incredible.' He was a hard taskmaster, but I loved it.

My hero at the time was Barry McGuigan. I was obsessed with watching his boxing technique on video and would play the same round numerous times over just to work out how he was throwing his punches. Barry was a great body puncher, a pressure fighter and had a crunching southpaw left hook. I wanted to be that good and look as impressive.

I was very lucky to have Ray. Apart from being a great trainer, he would always spend extra time with me whenever I asked him to practise a punch or a combination. After every training session, I used to sprint and get the medicine ball and ask him to hold it, so I could practise the body shot.

Ray would say, 'I'll give you 10 minutes Paul.' That would turn into quarter of an hour and then, 20 minutes and, before you knew it, we had been there for nearly an hour practicing the left hook again and again, perfecting the move, improving the speed. My boxing had become an obsession and it was that which would one day make me a champion.

I was now working with Ray far more on strategy and new angles than I'd ever done before. I not only wanted to be able to throw a punch, I wanted to step through the ropes with a game plan and have a series of feigns or steps in advance so that when it was unleashed my opponent was either off balance or their guard was down.

Although, sometimes I would get carried away, Ray would always let me have a go at something new. For example, I decided I wanted to use the screw shot, an unorthodox punch with is almost like a straight arm uppercut through the middle of the guard of your opponent, aiming under the chin.

At first he was apprehensive but I started to practise endlessly on the bags. Ray knew I was a perfectionist and when he saw me starting to land it successfully in competitions, he was delighted for me. Not for the punch itself but because I had dedicated so much of my time and energy to making a technique work and having self-belief.

****

I HAD received an incredible amount of support from my family and friends but the reality was that boxing was starting to cost me money – more than we could afford. Edgehill Community Centre raised about £300 to help me out and without Scarborough ABC I certainly couldn't have afforded to travel the length and breadth of the country.

The cost of new gloves, pads, gum shields, shorts, socks, food and so on started to add up and on top of all that I was still growing, so whatever I had one year wouldn't be usable the next and sometimes things didn't even last that long – and there was the food – cue Kevin Cowley.

Kevin was an ex-paratrooper who owned the Albion pub in Scarborough and was approached by someone who knew me, asking if he would act as a sponsor or knew of someone who might. Before agreeing to anything, Kevin asked if he could come to my house and meet me and my mum, just to make sure I was serious about boxing and that I was not just another 14-year-old going through a phase.

My first impression of Kevin was that he was a really nice guy, but he had come over to talk business and I wasn't prepared for that. He asked me a straight question, 'What are you looking for in terms of sponsorship? What do you need and I'll see if I can help.'

I was a shy kid who didn't want to offend his generosity and mumbled, 'Can I have a couple of T-shirts?' Kevin paused and I thought to myself, maybe I should have asked for just one. He replied, 'Ok – what else?' I said, 'That's all really' and he told me to leave it with him, shook our hands and left.

What happened next left me and mum speechless.

After leaving our house, he went straight down to the sports shop in town and explained to the owner that he wanted the best boxing gear he had in stock for an up-and-coming star.

He then drove straight back about and, without any fuss whatsoever, dumped about £300 worth of gear on our sofa and said, 'Work your way through that mate and let me know how you get on.'

We didn't know whether to laugh or cry.

His generosity didn't stop there, though. Over the years, as an amateur, every time I was fighting for England and had to travel – whether it was in the UK or abroad – he would always give me some cash. It wasn't that he was trying to be flash but he knew I came from a poor family and he just didn't want me getting embarrassed in front of the other lads because I might not be able to afford something.

Kevin never told anybody about his generosity towards me. Incredible.

****

BY the end of 1986, I had my sights firmly set on the NABCs (National Ambition Boxing Championship), the Junior ABAs and Young England. I was in terrific shape and well positioned but, unfortunately, my appendix had other plans. With only a few weeks to go before the competition, I had to have it taken out and was crying my eyes out to Tommy saying that this was my one big chance and it may never come again.

I even asked him if I could still box in the ABAs a few days after the op, but he calmly said, 'No, you'll get many other chances. Take a few weeks off to relax. I'm sure you will find something to keep you busy.'

I did, courtesy of my good mate Kenny who

mentioned he had two newborn lurcher puppies. He didn't have a garden, only a small backyard, so I came up with the idea of bringing them over to my place and we could share them as pets and hunting dogs.

Kenny said, 'Are you sure your mam will be ok with this?' I told him not to worry.

You should have seen her face when she walked into the kitchen to see this massive cage with two puppies under an ultraviolet light.

'What the hell is that?' she said. 'It can't stay here.' A few days later, she came in and noticed the cage had disappeared and said, 'Thanks for that. I know you loved those puppies.'

Then, looking out of the kitchen window, she saw a massive kennel in our small garden. She turned to me and said, 'I give up. You need to look after them though.' I was over the moon, as was Kenny.

A couple of months after my operation, I was back at the gym but now training with the adults full time. The atmosphere was buzzing in the club with some real characters about. Pro boxer Dougie Calderwood was one and another was 'Big' Phil Riley, who was not only a very good amateur boxer but an absolutely lovely bloke.

Although not world champions, these guys were a big help in making me train harder, be fitter and think clever in the ring. The other boxers were now treating me like an equal and it made me that little bit hungrier to justify it.

Ray would start us off with a warm-up and then send us off on a run. On our return we would do bag work and they'd match us up with somebody for a tough sparring session. Then we would finish off with the floor work; sit-ups, press-ups, more sit-ups, more press-ups, followed by speed work, pads and then we would cool down with stretching and light skipping. It would usually last about an hour. There was no messing about allowed and I loved every second of it.

Outside of the gym I wanted to train nonstop. It didn't matter if it was in the park, the garden, or doing my sprints in the local car park, I'd practise hour upon hour, working on my fitness, conditioning, technique, movement and power, every aspect of my game.

I trained like a machine and loved it and when an opportunity came up to exercise, I never missed it. John Amos used to repair washing machines in Filey, which was about eight miles away from our estate and I would tag along for the ride.

The first time he took me, he was chatting to the guy he was picking the machine up from when it started to rain really heavily. John was looking for me but after a few minutes soon realised I wasn't there.

I'd decided to run home. It took John about 20 minutes to get back to Edgehill and you should have seen his face when I rocked up about 20 minutes later dripping in sweat.

Ray would often say, 'Try and spar a level above your ability, so it's competitive.' There was a guy called George Rhodes, an awkward southpaw, who turned out to be a very good friend, and although he was older, stronger and bigger, I was able to use my boxing brain to make sure I didn't take any unnecessary punishment from him.

As the months of sparring progressed, we both started to step it up a little and after a couple of rounds you would hear people in the background saying, 'Those two are going for it.' On one occasion, my mum had come down to see us spar and had to walk out because we were both trying to knock each other out.

George was a real nice kid and the second we finished sparring we were back to being best of mates again. That's how it should always be in boxing. It's about learning a discipline, not street fighting.

He grew up on a tough estate not far from where I lived and was able to relate to how sport offered a sense of pride.

George now runs a boxing club on that same estate he grew up in, ploughing something back into the local community which took him under their wing as a kid and also helping out the future generation of champions who otherwise might have strayed off the straight and narrow. I couldn't be prouder of him. And to top it off, his son, George Rhodes Jr, has turned pro, after a glittering amateur career.

Another great sparring partner I had back then was a 23-year-old featherweight, Mark Legge, and over time we developed quite a bond. We spent many a weekend practising moves and techniques at the club, getting extra rounds in, and pushing each other on long runs.

Although a stone heavier than me, we were sparring partners for 10 years, completing over 300 rounds against each other. Like George, I owe a lot to Mark from those early days.

****

WITH my operation fully healed, I jumped back into competition, physically and mentally far stronger, and managed to do the double by winning the junior ABAs and NABCs in 1987. To say I was delighted was an understatement.

A year later, GCSEs were introduced and while some of my mates were then thinking about what line of work they might get into and the odd few considering 'A' levels, most of them were left scratching their heads thinking, 'What shall I do now?'

I had turned my back on the education system and didn't have anything to show for it. I did, however, have a stack of boxing trophies. But how far would that really get me?

'**Y**ou have broken the law
and could even be a sent
to prison.'
            - Court judge, 1990,
assessing Paul Ingle's case

Round 5
□
The Yorkshire Poacher

WHEN I left school at the age of 16, I realised that I'd need to get some extra cash otherwise I simply couldn't carry on with my boxing. The problem was, I had no idea where to start looking for work as I didn't really have any skills or qualifications. Thankfully I had a guardian angel in the background who was about to sort me out.

Up to that point, I didn't really know Ron Brown that well. I was aware he was the director of the local builder's yard, Sinclairs, and he was also my mum's cousin. Although we'd occasionally cross paths at family parties, he wasn't someone I would have approached for help.

Ron was an instantly recognisable character, standing six feet five and weighing 19 stone. But it wasn't his physical presence that got him known and respected in the local community, it was his good nature.

Little did I know, but Ron had got wind via some of the guys at his yard, that there was a promising young lad who was finding it hard to fit his boxing training in and get a job to pay for it.

When he found out that it was me, he called my mum up straight away and asked what the deal was. I remember overhearing the call and my mum saying to him, 'It's bloody hard to find a company that is willing to allow him to train with the England squad, attend the various camps, go abroad, and still pay him a wage. It's always at the back of his mind that he might not be able to achieve his goals in boxing, because he can't afford the equipment or the travel and he won't ask anybody for help.'

Before she could say much more, Ron told her to send me down there first thing in the morning. He also told her to pass me on a message, 'Tell Paul, in addition to giving him a job, my company will sponsor him, covering the costs associated with his boxing. If he has a clear mind, he can live his life a little bit more relaxed.'

Both mum and I were gobsmacked.

In all honesty, I was pretty nervous. Not only was it the first adult job I was taking on, but I didn't want to look like an idiot in front of family.

In order for me to become a general labourer, Ron sent me all round the firm, to help me understand what the construction business was about. I had about five mentors to teach me different skills such as bricklaying, plastering, plumbing, electricity, driving and delivering. They were also there to give me a verbal clip round the ear when I wasn't pulling my weight.

Outside the ring, the only real discipline I'd experienced up to that point was limited, the school timetable, which I'd tried to get around as often as not.

At times, shovelling tarmac and laying kerbs for hours on end was tough but I'm sure it helped to build my upper body strength.

Over the years there have been a number of fighters

who have had to do the same, Marvin Hagler and Tony Sibson were both hod carriers.

As I began to win more and more, I needed to be away at regular training camps and when I was back at work I'd often be knackered.

Ron started to give me work that didn't need any long-term commitment, the kind of jobs I could step away from and anybody could finish off the day after. The lads never moaned once. In fact, if I was in the middle of a training camp, they would often let me sleep in the back of the van for a couple of hours to recharge my batteries and do my share of the work. I owe them all a lot, especially Ron as he turned a blind eye to a number of my antics, well, the ones he was aware of.

As soon as I turned 17, in the hot summer of 1989, I went out and bought my first transport and applied for my provisional driving licence.

It was a Mini van which I'd bought locally for a bargain price and within days it started acting up. It was always breaking down and I'm sure that John Amos spent more time under it doing repairs than I did driving it.

When it did work though, I loved it. The back had been ripped out and decked with red fur throughout and big fluffy dice hanging from the mirror. Driving down the Scarborough seafront with my windows wound down and my £40 stereo blasting away was as good as it could get.

The van might have seemed a tiny bit tacky to some, but with the inbuilt lounge at the back coming as standard, the car was very popular with my mates, with them wanting to borrow it at weekends.

One day Ron noticed I was now driving to work and passed me the keys to one of the company Escort vans. Neither of us thought anything of it.

About three months later he asked, 'I don't seem to have a copy of your driver's licence on file which I need for the fleet insurance.' I handed it over and he erupted. 'What's this,' he spluttered. 'It's a provisional licence. You shouldn't be driving my van, your van or anything with an engine. The only way you are getting back in is with 'L' plates and an instructor.' Two driving tests later I was back in the driving seat – legally.

What Ron also didn't know was that whilst waiting for my first few sets of wages to come through, I was absolutely broke but still wanted to be cruising the seafront in the Mini van.

On a couple of occasions, I siphoned some petrol from the company van to keep mine going for a few days. There was no science behind the act. I used to stick a piece of hosepipe into the tank, suck it up and on more than one occasion would get covered in fuel or get a mouthful.

At the end of the week we had to fill out a mileage book and the petrol we'd used. The guy looking at the number of miles versus fuel consumption couldn't understand why mine didn't tally. Before he cottoned on I mentioned, 'That van does really shitty miles to the gallon. You might want to get it seen to.' He seemed grateful.

I wanted to tell Ron, but after a while it became more and more uncomfortable.

****

THAT year also contained some momentous milestones in my amateur boxing career, including winning the silver medal in the flyweight multi-nations in Sardinia.

It was my first taste of going abroad and one of my lasting memories is not so much the boxing, but the food. I'm not sure if they were trying to fatten us up, but the quality and varieties of pasta available was something else. If we had been there for a couple more days I would have come back as a light heavyweight.

Boxing as a senior now for the England squad was a big step up, not least with coach, Ian Irwin. He wasn't a dictator, he was always very respectful but he always reminded us that being on his team would require an incredible amount of discipline and dedication, which would only be achieved if we listened to instructions.

Sometimes I would spend a few weeks at a camp down at Crystal Palace in London and at the end of it Ian would give me a training schedule to practise and Ray Simpson back home would make sure I did exactly what was needed. I was very lucky to have great coaches on both sides of the fence.

One thing that became clear as I joined the England team was that I wasn't a great lover of travelling or, more to the point, leaving Scarborough – I'm a home bird.

In the early days of being on the squad, I put my place in jeopardy due to my stubbornness and in all honesty, stupidity. On my initial visits training with the squad in London, I think I was a little culture-shocked.

I'd been brought up among folk who would say hello when they walked past on the street or stop for a chat even if they didn't know me too well.

On the streets of London, especially in the areas we were training, I knew no one and everybody was always in a hurry. It was a very cold and odd contrast.

The other difference I noticed when getting up for my early morning runs was the air. I used to run on the beach in Scarborough or up the hills and, with the amount of oxygen my lungs would take in, I'd come back home feeling fantastic.

Running on the streets of East London with hundreds of cars was simply not the same. I'd often blow my nose after a run and black dirt would be left on the tissue.

In my eyes, I saw nothing wrong with not wanting to travel to London and had it not been for my coaches, my boxing career may well have come to an end at that moment.

Tommy was the first to pick up on my antics. On one occasion I was due to train at Crystal Palace and I turned up at the gym in Scarborough. He asked what I was doing there and I told him that the train hadn't turned up.

He looked at me and let it slide, but he could tell I was lying. He said, 'Ok, but next time, even if you've missed the train, find another way there, even if you have to walk. There are kids out there who would give their right arm to be on that squad and you could get thrown off if you don't attend.'

I was a little shaken but an hour later thought nothing of it. In my eyes it was no different to playing the same bus trick in front of Irene's shop which I used to get away with as a kid.

Tommy got chatting with Ray and explained what I'd done and then Ray in turn called Ian Irwin, who was none too happy. Ian enquired at the station and found out that the train had run 10 minutes late and got in touch with me straight away. In under 30 seconds he laid it on the line.

'Do you want to be on the squad?' he stressed 'If you do, you need to be present at training as and when the camps are and wherever they are, do you understand? There will be no second chances from here on in and if you pull the same stunt again, you're off the squad. I don't care how much talent you have, your attitude could rub off on the others and I won't have that happening on this team.'

I was genuinely shaken up. When I'd skived anything before, there were no serious consequences. A slapped wrist and a lecture, maybe, but nothing I cared about. This was totally different.

In the space of a quick phone conversation I suddenly realised that my stubbornness could put my dream in jeopardy. Everything I'd worked for since the age of seven, everything I'd sacrificed could disappear in a heartbeat. That was the last time I missed any training camp ever again. I had just turned a massive corner.

Eventually I got into the swing of long-distance training and, to soften the blow, I started travelling with two team-mates and good friends, Peter Richardson and Anthony Todd. We would meet at Doncaster train station and travel to wherever required. I was fully focused again.

****

SOME people used to joke that I might have made a great swimmer from a young age, due to being born with webbed toes and flat feet. The middle two toes on both my feet are connected and although I have a similarity to a duck, I certainly don't move around in the water like one.

I'd managed to get through my boxing career at that point without anyone seeing any issues with my feet but when you start boxing at national and international level, you have a great number of eyes constantly checking you, especially coaches and doctors.

One day, whilst at a training camp with the England squad, one of the coaches saw me coming in from a long run wearing my usual trainers and was horrified.

'What are they? Slippers?' he said. 'You can't train in them anymore Paul.' Up to that point I ran in my ordinary trainers, which were more fashionable than anything, but were never meant for distance.

The Yorkshire Hunter

We were a poor family, so they were also my going out shoes – I was wearing them about five hours a day. Those trainers had cost me about twenty quid but what I really needed was a proper pair which cost about £100.

The truth was, having webbed feet and being flat footed, I needed something with major support and mine simply didn't provide that. The idea was to raise the arch so it was in the middle of my foot, which would help me when I was running and would also reduce my back pain.

You would have thought that when the squad gave me a top pair of trainers with insoles I would have been delighted, but I wasn't. They felt tight, awkward, massive on my feet and the pain they were causing was unbelievable.

I put up with the insoles for a couple of years, but as the quality of footwear improved, I was able to find boxing boots and running trainers which naturally provided me with ample support and gladly ditched them.

****

JOINING the British boxing squad was more than just sport. With the number of international tournaments I took part in, I was able to visit some incredible countries including Italy, Denmark, Finland, Australia, Czech Republic, USA, Spain and Canada.

Being given the opportunity to see some of the local culture was first class. There was, however, one country that made a longer-lasting impression on me. That was Peru when I was fighting in the 1990 world championships.

When we arrived at our hotel in Lima, it banished all the negatives mentioned before we left the UK. It was as clean as a whistle, the food was immaculate and the staff bent over backwards if we asked for anything. It was very humbling.

The next morning, we headed off to the gym which had a fantastic atmosphere and were greeted by the Peruvian team, who instantly asked if they could swap tracksuits.

It was an open air venue and just how I liked it – rough and ready. What were set up as punch bags were worn out, the pads had seen better days and the equipment in general gave you the impression that it was on its last legs.

The British ambassador came to watch us train and, as he stepped out of the car, the bodyguards waiting to greet him opened their jackets to reveal their guns. You should have seen the faces on Team GB. We'd never seen anything like it before and it added to the atmosphere of this mysterious country.

The only problem with the gym was that each country had an allocated slot on a rota and that time could not be moved. Ian wanted us training at the exact time when we would be competing, which wasn't always possible.

He was very resourceful, though, and would pinch any inch of space for the squad to train in, which included a corner of the yard at the back of the hotel, or clearing out one of our hotel rooms so we could do some skipping, shadow boxing and pad work.

Outside, on the streets, we were genuinely knocked back by how poor it was. Frighteningly poor. After a couple of days, a guide took us for a walk into some of the small towns and it was pretty scary stuff. Everywhere we went, small kids begged and injured animals dragged themselves along the floor or were dead on the side of the road and, by the look of it, had been there for a while. Each time we went into a café, people would be staring at us eating, partly because they were hungry themselves and partly because they were fascinated with the strangers from out of town. It was pretty unnerving, added to by the local delicacy being deep fried guinea pig.

It was as common as fish and chips out there and they were wolfing it down – head, claws, the lot. I gave it a miss.

As poor as they were, they were very proud and honest people. Ian gave one of the cleaners a bottle of booze he'd picked up from Duty Free and she had to come back and get a signature from him to take back to the authorities to prove that she hadn't stolen it.

The rest of us left tips for the staff and gave away T-shirts and some other bits of kit and when I was leaving the maid was so touched, so she took a picture of the Virgin Mary off the wall and gave it to me. That was all she had.

Despite boxing really smoothly at the world championships there, I lost a close decision in the semi-final and came away with a bronze medal. I was crying with rage afterwards as I knew the gold should have been mine. It was all part of the learning process and my grit and determination kept me focused for the next challenge on the horizon.

Soon after returning, I focused on the flyweight ABA title. I was quite well established on the amateur circuit by this stage and my shorts told the tale as they were covered with badges back and front from the various competitions I'd fought in. After getting through the opening rounds, I went on to win the quarter finals in Colchester and then fought the Scottish champion called Neil Armstrong in the semis in Blackpool. I knocked him down in the first and stopped him in the second. In all honesty it was an easy fight.

The support from the fans at the resort was massive and quite a few of my mates had come up to watch me.

My sparring partner Mark Legge had made the journey and after the fight I asked him, 'Where are you staying tonight?' He told me, 'I haven't got anywhere. I'll find somewhere.' I said, 'When Tommy Johnson goes to bed, you can crash on the floor in my room.'

In the morning, I told Mark, 'Why don't you go down for breakfast as I don't fancy it, just bring me up an orange juice. You need to go early, though, before Tommy comes downstairs and you'll have to pretend to be me when they ask for your name in the dining room.'

He went downstairs and when asked his name by the restaurant manager he said, 'Paul Ingle' and the whole room turned around to look and then people starting walking over and shaking his hand and patting him on the back congratulating him on his performance the night before.

They started asking him, 'How old are you?' and he told them, 17, although he was 24 at the time. One of them noted straight away, 'You look very mature', at which point he swiftly grabbed my glass of juice, made his way back up to the room and told me the whole story. I was laughing my head off when I heard.

Unfortunately, I lost in the final against Johnny Armour at the Albert Hall in London. It was the first time I'd worn a head guard and I couldn't stand it.

It was like putting a muzzle on a dog for the first time. I spent most of the fight wanting to tear it off because it didn't feel right and kept slipping down over my eyes.

The fight between us was pretty close going into the third and final round, until I was given a standing eight count and had a point deducted for holding within the space of about 20 seconds.

Despite giving Johnny a bloodied nose and a good run for his money, he was simply too seasoned a fighter for me at that point. Johnny was 21 and turned pro a few months later and continued to have a good career, winning the Commonwealth, European and WBU titles.

Soon after the Armour fight I came across my toughest opponent as an amateur when I took on a

Lithuanian boxer in the European championships in Czechoslovakia. He was the most demoralising fighter I'd ever come across. He stood square in front of me but always seemed to be a little bit out of distance for me to tag him. His hand speed and accuracy was unbelievable – I just couldn't get to him. It was as if he could see me coming in slow motion and had an answer for everything.

Every time I moved forward to get near him, he would take a step back and catch me, like a meerkat with a cobra. Very clever, very awkward. I remember going back to the corner after the first round saying, 'Everything he throws he catches me with and I can't nail him. I'm feigning before I throw a punch and he catches me, I'm feigning when moving away, and he catches me.'

I'd never encountered a fighter who could read me before. After three rounds I was knackered. He went on to win that tournament. Funny thing is, after that, I never saw him again.

****

THE year 1990 certainly gave me a great deal of publicity as a boxer but unfortunately I was about to make the headlines for the wrong reasons.

When I started boxing, I was always told that fish was an excellent source of protein. However, with our limited resources, I started to think about where else I could get it from. Then somebody I knew told me where I could fish for trout, but that I'd need a licence. I heard the first part clearly but was not so good on the second.

I started fishing when I was about 14 and used to go most weekends with some good mates. In an attempt to hide the trout from any fishing officers, I'd put them in my jacket pockets, my trousers and even my wellies. When I got home it was pretty obvious to my mum where I had been as I absolutely stank of fish but she didn't know the half of it.

I used to sell most of my fish to the local restaurants to make some pocket money but sometimes I'd struggle with what to do with my catch. On one occasion I'd caught a scary 13lb pike with a full set of sharp teeth and really didn't know who would take it.

I walked into the house, pulled it out of my bag and hung it on the back of the kitchen door. Mum looked horrified, she thought it was a shark. I then went upstairs to change my stinking clothes and when I came back down, the fish suddenly moved. We ran out of the kitchen and it took us about 10 minutes before we had the courage to go back in.

One particular morning, I went fishing with a good mate of mine around 5am and we started catching three and four pound freshwater trout using our cheap telescopic fishing rods with a lump of bread on a hook. Next to us were fly fishers with all the flash gear, who never caught a thing.

We'd caught about three or four at this point but only had one on display when, suddenly, this guy jumped out of a bush and said in a very official voice, 'Have you got your fishing licence with you?'

We froze and, unlike me, I didn't know what to say. I mumbled, 'Of course, but I've left it at home.' The guy replied, 'No problem. If you give me your name and home address, I can confirm that. If you don't have a licence then you shouldn't be here because that's poaching and it's illegal.'

I gave him a fake address and then about an hour later drove home. What I didn't realise, was that the fishing official had taken down my number plate as I drove off.

About three weeks later I got a visit from the police whilst at work at Sinclairs. First thing that went through my mind was that something had happened to my mum or brother and they had come with bad news. They asked if I remembered fishing in Forge Valley and to see my licence. I said, 'I've lost it,' but they were ahead of the game and told me that there were no records of me ever having bought one and that I could be in some serious trouble.

My first thought was that mum would kill me and immediately I got home I told her about it. She went mad. I was trying to be keep calm but she was furious. 'That's a serious offence, Paul' she also said. 'What were you thinking? You could get locked away for this!' Now I was worried.

Sure enough, I ended up in court. I took all the blame because at the time I was the one with a rod in my hand and was happy that my mate didn't have to get in trouble. He offered to pay half the fine; I'm still waiting.

The way the judge was talking, you'd have thought I'd killed somebody. It was one fish. When he said, 'You have broken the law and could even be sent to prison,' I started to get seriously concerned. After a short adjournment, the judge decided, 'You have been granted a six month conditional discharge. If you are found guilty again during that period you will have to go to a detention centre.'

I was not quite 18 at the time so my mum had to come with me but that was certainly a bonus. The judge at first wanted me to pay £250 at £5 per week, but she told him we couldn't afford it.

They were locked in a stare but mum is made of strong stuff and wasn't getting bullied by anybody. In the end she got the judge down to a £76 fine at £2 per week.

The day after, the press picked up on the story and were having a field day. Little did they know, it wasn't the only licence I didn't have. I drove to the fishing without one as well.

The truth is, I had about 15 trout in my bag on the day I was rumbled and had been fishing at that spot for a few years so, in all honesty, it could have been a lot worse.

****

AT the ABA final against Johnny Armour, BBC television commentator Harry Carpenter said, 'Ingle is a brave runner-up and his time will come soon.' It wasn't long.

In 1991, I came back a stronger, more seasoned and confident fighter and became the amateur flyweight champion, beating Michael Horobin at the Albert Hall. Michael was about four years older than me, had also been on the England squad and was a strong, determined fighter.

A few months after, I flew off to Ottawa to fight in the Canada Cup and not only won the gold medal but also the best boxer of the tournament. With my sweat barely dried, I packed my suitcase once again and headed to Sydney for the world championships.

I was looking forward to seeing Australia and spending three weeks with the squad, but my love of flying hadn't got any better and being up in the air for 20-something hours with two stops along the way didn't help things out.

Touring the set of *Neighbours* and visiting the Opera House and the harbour with the likes of Peter Ridgeon, Jon Irwin, Robin Reid and Peter Richardson made the whole experience a lot of fun, but unfortunately, my quest to get back-to-back gold medals was cut short when I was beaten in the quarter finals. In fact, none of the boxers on the squad on this occasion came away with a medal.

Unlike others on the team who decided to ditch the amateur game at that point, I was far from done. I was about to take part in the tournament which all amateurs dream of.

> '**I** would have loved to been able to hold Paul for another Olympics. I'm sure he would have won a medal – most likely gold.'
> - *Ian Irwin,*
> *Team GB Head Boxing Coach*

Round 6

□

Barcelona

I CARRIED on working at Sinclairs builders yard until I was 19, but it was becoming more and more obvious that if I wanted to succeed in boxing, something would have to give. I decided to meet with Ron and explain my position.

'I'm going to be away a lot longer now, a few weeks at a time and possibly a few months. I just don't think I'll be able to work here anymore and I wanted to say thank you for everything. I'll never forget it,' I told him.

Ron said, without making any fuss, 'If you need to come back, even just for a couple of days to get a few quid, I'll make sure something will be there waiting. I also intend to keep on sponsoring you until a point you and your mum are not having to worry about the financial side of things. Continue to make Scarborough proud with your boxing Paul.'

I was speechless. Genuinely touched. I didn't think people like this existed.

After leaving Sinclairs, I did the odd bit of ducking and diving to earn a few quid, such as window cleaning with

The Yorkshire Hunter

Kenny. Well, it was always me up the ladders cleaning, with Kenny footing them. I'm not sure if he had a fear of heights, water or hard graft.

Window cleaning was certainly not my focus as I was getting ready for the most prestigious tournament an amateur boxer could take part in.

****

THE first Olympics I can really remember was in 1984. Although I wasn't really up to speed with the boxers back then, the main star of the show was the sprinter Carl Lewis, who went on to win four gold medals.

By the next one, I was 16-years-old and had racked up a few titles and paid far more attention to the boxing in Seoul.

A Korean won the flyweight division and a few key names were touted as future world champions, including Lennox Lewis, Richie Woodhall, Riddick Bowe, Ray Mercer and Roy Jones Jr, who was on the end of one of the worst judging decisions ever, costing him the gold medal.

Inspired by the atmosphere that came with the competition, I had set myself the goal of competing at the next Olympics in 1992. However, getting there came with its own mini drama.

From what I and most of the boxing team understood from previous Olympics, if you impressed enough during the build up to the tournament by competing at international level and winning enough silverware, you would be in with a good chance for selection.

Unfortunately, that was not the case here.

We each had to fight in a qualification tournament and finish in the top four.

I fought in Copenhagen, Robin Reid went to Italy and some boxed in Finland.

Not being a great fan of flying either, mum never came out to see me fight outside British shores. The Danish tournament was not covered on television or radio and she stayed at home the whole day, sitting next to the phone, waiting for my call.

Later that evening she heard me shouting down the phone, 'I won the silver, I've got through. I'm going to the Olympics!'

Little did I know, but she'd gone straight round to all her friends and family and by the time I got home I had a gang of press at the front door wanting interviews and photographs. It was a little overwhelming, but also a special moment to cherish.

****

ARRIVING in Barcelona was something else. With such a buzz surrounding the event, Ian Irwin became very protective of us, to make sure we didn't get too carried away with the distractions.

The first night we were all invited to a pre-opening ceremony barbecue to get to meet the other athletes and major officials involved with putting on the games. However, before entering any area of the Olympic village, you had to pass through tight security, similar to an airport.

Whilst in the queue with Peter Richardson, Robin Reid and a few of the other lads, we suddenly noticed this massive bloke with ginger hair standing in front of us and loads of people wanting to have their photo taken with him or get his autograph. It was none other than Boris Becker, who was also competing at the games.

After a while, he turned to us and asked which sport we did and we told him we were the Great Britain boxing team.

Peter then turned to Boris and said, 'So what sport do you do mate?' Loads of people started laughing but Boris wasn't amused as he walked off through the security barrier.

The barbecue was fantastic. Not that me or the lads got to taste much of the food as we had to keep a strict eye on our weight, but we enjoyed the evening for the people in attendance and the fact that we were a part of that whole crew.

Led in by team captain Linford Christie, one of the first people we met was Princess Anne, who was really down to earth and then we met a few members of the Spanish royal family, who were extremely hospitable.

We got the chance to chat with all the Team GB athletes, including Sally Gunnell, Steve Backley and Colin Jackson. They were really chilled out and extremely polite. I was delighted when both Sally and Linford went on to win gold medals.

We then started to mingle with the other teams including the Americans who had some great fighters such as Oscar De La Hoya, Vernon Forrest, Montell Griffin and Chris Byrd, who were all down to earth and would go on to become great pro world champions.

The boxer we all wanted to speak to, who had come to support his fellow countrymen, was Evander Holyfield. At the time, Evander was the WBA, WBC and IBF world heavyweight champion and was the god of the boxing world.

I walked over and shook his hand and our conversation was almost comical.

As I introduced myself, Evander said, 'I beg your pardon?'

I then repeated myself and he asked, 'Where do you come from?'

I replied, 'I'm sorry. I didn't get that. What was your question?'

He repeated it and I told him Scarborough.

He said, 'Where?'

By then, both the USA and British boxing teams had burst into laughter as it became obvious that our respective accents were just not meant for each other.

A few days later, my uncle John and good mate Neil Cox also had the pleasure of chatting with Evander and when he asked them where they came from, he said excitedly, 'I met one of your guys the other day. Didn't understand him either.'

The day after, it started to dawn on me that I was part of the biggest sports show on the planet. Putting on my Team GB tracksuit with the big accreditation pass around my neck was the best uniform in the world. People started coming up to me shaking my hand and I hadn't even fought yet.

I felt incredible. I'd been through so much to get there and was so pumped up by the atmosphere just on the first morning that I was ready to jump in the ring and fight right at that moment.

As we walked into the athletes food court, the smell of fresh baked bread and a display of the finest food I'd ever seen was on display at no cost, 24/7. Most of us weren't scheduled to fight for about 10 days and had to really resist the temptation. To make it worse, you could smell the food from our bedrooms. I went to sleep on a number of occasions dreaming about the buffets.

We had to get suited and booted in preparation for the opening ceremony.

In all honesty, this was one of the toughest parts of

the Olympics for the British team. We'd all been given matching suits, boater hats and shiny shoes that were so tough, they didn't bend.

Having put all the gear on, we had to wait in an area underneath the seating of the stadium, until our country was called up, which in our case was a couple of hours away.

It was 35 degrees Celsius, with no wind blowing and we had enough clothing on to keep us warm in a snow storm. We soon started to moan and asked Ian Irwin if we could take the jackets and hats off, to no avail.

Finally, we got the call and started the walk out onto the running track at which point we realised we were pretty much the only ones not wearing short-sleeve shirts, shorts and certainly no boater hats.

The only benefit of wearing all that gear was that it kept me down to weight. It was like going for a run with the bin liners for two and a half hours and, by the end of it, my feet were on fire.

Thankfully, those memories were taken over by the magic of the opening ceremony. Walking into the stadium with Team GB, with loud music playing and a sea of people applauding and snapping away with their cameras was something I'll never forget.

Unfortunately, for my friends and family watching on television back home, trying to spot the small guy among a group of six footers was near on impossible.

****

ALTHOUGH we were able to wander out of the Olympic village if we wanted to, in the days leading up to my fights, I never did. I was quite content chilling with my mates swimming, playing tennis or bowling.

It wasn't all fun and games, though, as I was having to monitor my weight twice a day and the day before my fight it would be hourly.

I'd started to notice my body was changing and that I needed to seriously consider moving up and out of the flyweight division.

Up to this point I'd never struggled to make weight. I was never more than a couple of pounds over and managed to keep on top of it with my exercise regime and the odd sweat session, but I was now starting to realise that I needed to do that plus some to stay at the eight stone limit.

Training with Peter Richardson was fantastic because he was two years older and could educate me on how my body was starting to build more muscle as I got older, which in turn was adding weight to my frame.

When I first started training with him he was a featherweight and soon moved up to light welterweight, so he was also able to advise me on how to adjust. Like me, he only had to look at food and he'd pile on the pounds, so we ended up training together a great deal, especially in the days leading up to fights.

The heat in Barcelona was unbearable and it was essential not to get dehydrated.

My uncles, John and Alex, travelled out with some of my good friends and were staying in Lloret de Mar, about 80km north. They arrived a few days after me and once they'd settled, decided to get the train down to see the opening bouts.

On arriving in Barcelona in the 40 degree midday sun and cloudless sky, they spotted a sign which they thought was for the boxing, but couldn't understand why the area looked like a ghost town.

Spotting a Spaniard across the road, they asked him

where the boxing was, pointing to the sign. He looked back at them a little strangely. My good friend Neil Cox then started trying to do an impression of a boxer, throwing a few punches into the air and saying, 'Boxing, boxing', increasingly loudly.

The local understood them perfectly, but was just left bemused. After about 30 seconds he suddenly said, 'No boxing, badminton here. Boxing in Badalona, not Barcelona,' and pointed down the street.

They assumed that it must have been just up the road and started walking. Little did they know it was 13 kilometres away, and they got severely lost.

It took them most of the day to get to the arena, by which time, two of the lads had passed out from heat exhaustion and they were all burnt to a crisp.

When I met them outside, they looked like six escaped convicts who had just crossed the desert; cracked lips, hankies on their heads and empty bottles of water in their hands. To top it off, the boxing had just finished for the day.

I felt a bit sorry for Neil, so I lent him my special edition Ray-Ban Olympic sunglasses I'd been given. I next saw them again 21 years later.

The drama didn't stop there. The day after, they made the trek from Lloret once again but this time to Badalona direct, without any detours.

However, the lot of them had come to the Games without tickets, thinking it would be like watching a local football match back home in Scarborough and would be able to buy them on the door as they'd always done.

The USA basketball 'Dream Team' were also playing at the same venue, so there were thousands of people queuing up waiting to get in.

Above: First row, far left. Already focused on training later that day...

Left: Being a Yorkshireman a love of cricket is a no-brainer. I'm front row, far right.

Right: Dwarfed by my football team. I'm back row, far left.

Above: Starting to clock up the silverware as a junior...   *Scarborough News*

Left: As kids in Scarborough, biking on Edgehill estate.

Below: Me and my brother Dean doing the Ingle double.

Right: I was also quite handy with a table tennis bat in my youth.

Below: Testing out my uppercut...

Right: The medal that got me into the Olympics. Copenhagen 1992.

Above and right: Washing... and drying... during the Barcelona Olympics.

Left: Bang on the eight-stone limit, fighting fit and ready to rumble before, *above*, beating Alex Baba in the first round at the 1992 Olympics.

Above: Robin Reid can't resist a photo bomb in Barcelona. Ahead of his time.

Right: I was the underdog going into my first title fight...

Left: Proud neighbours eaglerly await my return to Edgehill with flags, when I became British champion, January 1997.

Below: Getting ready to fight Jon Jo Irwin for the Commonwealth title in November 1997.

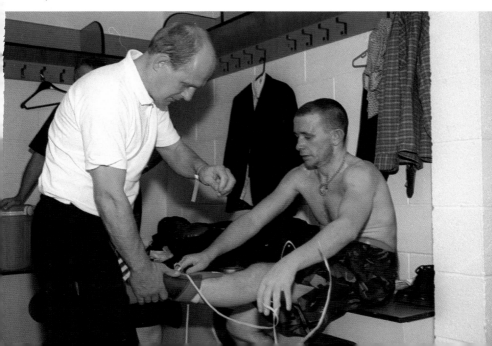

Left: As British champion, facing up to challenger Michael Alldis.

Below: Giving the Lonsdale belt to my mum as promised.

Right: Ready to defend the Commonwealth strap against Trust Ndlovu, March 1998.

Above: Training with Toncho Tonchev ahead of my European title challenge.

Above: The Moussa Sangare press conference with boxers left to right - Toncho Tonchev, Darren Christie, Terry Morrill, me and Tony Booth.

Above: Kickboxer Mark Elwood celebrates the opening of his refurbished Tornado Gym on Madeley Street, Hessle Road with my help. I used to train at the gym.

Left and above: Celebrating Christmas 1998 - and it's fireworks on Bonfire Night too!

Just as they started to panic, a cagy-looking Spaniard came up to them and asked which events they wanted to see. They were all very wary and had been warned about forgeries before going out, so, they did the sensible thing and decided to ask him for six tickets to the boxing.

The guy took off one of his shoes and pulled out a wad of tickets and charged them 1,000 pesetas less than face value. They now started to fear the worst as they approached the tight security barriers, but in the end they just flashed their tickets and strolled on through with big smiles on their faces.

The atmosphere in the boxing arena was unbelievable and the camaraderie among the boxing team was something else. When one of our number was up, we were screaming our heads off.

It was fantastic watching my mate, underdog Peter Richardson take on and beat future world professional champion Vernon Forrest, who he'd lost to at the world championships in Sydney the year before, 14-8. The place erupted.

In Seoul in 1988, the Olympic committee had introduced headguards, which was not very popular with many fighters, but they went one better for the Barcelona games. At the 11th hour, they decided to bring in a computerised scoring system which, in all honesty, was a nightmare.

The reaction from all the boxers and trainers from around the world was not good. We simply didn't have enough time to practise with the system in training and it became something of an absolute lottery as to who was going to win.

Even the supporters started to become quieter as the points were being racked up, as they couldn't see who was scoring and why. They should have tried being in the ring, it made even less sense.

The main target became the head, but power was not a consideration. You could literally touch your opponent's face with a feather and it was counted as a point. Knockdowns became almost extinct and body punches were only credited if an opponent was dispatched to the canvas.

Both the guards and the computerised scoring method have now gone, over 20 years too late in my opinion.

First up, I was fighting a tough Ghanaian by the name of Alex 'Ali' Baba. I've always been a bit nervous before my fights, especially the big ones, but for some reason, the occasion surrounding this one was really starting to get to me.

I decided to have a chat with Robin Reid, who by now I knew very well from having fought all over the world with him for the previous four years. I asked him how he handled such a stage and the pressure. He told me just to look on it as any other tournament and to realise what I'd achieved in them – more than him, he reminded me.

Thankfully that little chat helped calm me down and I was ready to tear into Baba. I'd already faced him a few months earlier in Ottawa and beaten him. He was a very strong kid and it didn't matter what you hit him with it would bounce off. The strategy was pretty simple – move forward in straight lines and come off at angles.

By the end of the second round I was four points up and Ian Irwin calmly said, 'Stay in range but don't get knocked about. There are three minutes to go and the rest of the tournament ahead of you, so we don't want to see you pick up an injury. Ok? Keep it tight, tidy and accurate.'

It wasn't a breeze, but I certainly knew that I had done enough by the end of the third and final round to win, or so

I thought. Although I felt like I'd landed about 500 punches and most of his were to my kidneys, the computer only scored the contest 9-7 in my favour. A bit too close for comfort.

My next fight, two days later, was against a North Korean called Choi Chol-Su, who was in your face all the time. When I hit him, he would be right there ready to throw another punch and there was no opportunity to make a mistake or take your eyes off the target.

Always easier in hindsight, but I shouldn't have fought him the way I did.

The advice I'd being given in the corner was to keep on the back foot but it soon became obvious that getting in close and giving him some stick was working far better, so I stuck with my strategy.

Going into the last round, Ian Irwin never told me the exact score, but he knew I was down by six points, with Choi winning 10-4. He said, 'You're down Paul and the way the computer is scoring you it will be a tough climb. You need a good round.'

I was absolutely gobsmacked as I'd hit him with everything but the kitchen sink and he'd only caught me with some glancing shots. I thought I was miles ahead.

I went out there and enjoyed myself for the last three minutes. When the scores were announced on the microphone as 13-12 to Choi, I was devastated. The crowd started booing, which also gave an indication of how they thought the contest had gone.

The main problem for us was not knowing what I had scored with. I couldn't tell you if the 12 points I bagged were unintentional shots I threw trying to get out of the way of a punch, or if it was from a clean attack. It made no sense.

Seven months of training and competition fighting

over the last four years to arrive at the Olympics and I was edged out by a point. The only slight consolation was that Choi went on to win the gold.

In the end, only one of us from Team GB won a medal. Robin Reid claimed the middleweight bronze and we were all ringside to cheer him on. I was dead chuffed as he's a great lad and became super middleweight champion of the world later on in his pro career.

Nevertheless, from a team perspective it was disappointing.

We had one of the best crop of fighters in years, it was the first time in English Olympic history at that point that 11 boxers had qualified to fight there.

Ian Irwin was an absolute rock after I walked off the ring apron. He knew I was gutted losing by a whisker and told me, 'You boxed the best you could and nobody can ever say that you did not give it everything for this Olympics. Whatever you are doing you need a bit of lady luck in life. It went with Choi this time. Yours will come.'

It was just the boost I needed and I'll always be grateful to him for saying what he did immediately after the fight.

After an incredible closing ceremony and a once in a lifetime adventure, I headed back home with the squad. On my return to Scarborough, I had decided I wanted to make a visit to someone special.

Kevin Cowley had supported me in my early days by buying me equipment and always slipped me a few quid whenever I travelled abroad but never wanted anything in return. I'd often ask if I could help promote his pub, but he was never interested.

A couple of days after getting back from Barcelona I went round there and saw him behind the bar. I could see he was busy but leaned over and said, 'I've got something and wondered if you might like it though I'm not even sure if you'll want it.'

I picked up my bag and could see Kevin waiting in anticipation. I pulled the zip back and reached inside and handed him one of my Olympic boxing vests that I'd used at the games.

He was speechless and had a tear in his eye as I told him, 'It would be my honour for you to accept it.'

Without the support from the likes of Kevin and many other generous people in Scarborough, I may have never worn that vest in the first place. I'll never forget where I came from.

****

THE only other marginal benefit of not progressing past Choi was that I was able to get stuck into the buffet for a couple of days although my competition fighting that year was far from over.

A couple of months after Barcelona, I was back on a plane to Ottawa and competed in the Canada Cup again. I'd won the gold medal and best boxer of the tournament the year before and was absolutely over the moon when I did exactly the same again this time around.

Doing the double back to back focused me for my last year of amateur competition.

Having taken an enforced absence from the ABAs because of the Olympics, I was in incredible condition for them in '93.

I had a great training camp but a week before the competition I was struck with some bad news.

The man who had taken me under his wing and

guided me like a son through my early boxing days passed away.

Paddy Govier was 85 and had lived his life exactly how he wanted. He not only made his dreams come true but influenced so many kids in Scarborough to make themselves better people through boxing. I was devastated.

I publicly announced that I was going to win the flyweight title as a tribute to him and thankfully was able to keep my promise.

My opponent in the final was Paul Shepherd who was a good strong fighter but, and taking nothing away from him, I found him very predictable and I'm sure Paddy was looking down on me sending me all the luck.

The final test of my amateur career came in an international tournament held in Berlin, where I was the only English boxer chosen to represent Europe against a team from the USA. My team mates included some outstanding fighters such as future world champs Sven Ottke and Kostya Tszyu, and it was inspiring to be able to train alongside these guys in the weeks before, as we were constantly pushing each other.

The atmosphere stepping out into the Berlin arena was immense. There were just under 20,000 fans cheering us on and every time a European fighter was making their ring entrance, it felt like the roof was going to come off.

I'm glad to say I won my last amateur international contest very comfortably on points. I was so far ahead by the end of the second round, that Ian Irwin was worried I might relax and reminded me to keep sharp and not leave it to the judges.

With the Choi memories still fresh, I boxed that last round like everything depended on it and when the decision was announced, I had won by a mile.

I knew that I wanted to turn pro. I'd achieved a great deal since the age of 11, the camaraderie involved with boxing at national and international levels was unbelievable, not to mention being sponsored to travel the world.

I was very aware that turning pro was a solo sport and all those years I'd spent with some great guys was about to finish. Looking back, they were the best days of my life.

I would also be taking huge physical and financial risks stepping into the pro ranks and would have to start from scratch in terms of getting a new team around me. I ultimately knew where I wanted to be long term, but had no idea how to start the journey.

'**W**hen you drop your
guard in films, the
acting process
compensates.'
- *Sir Ben Kingsley,
arguably Scarborough's most
famous acting name*

'**W**hen you drop your
guard in the ring,
you get knocked out.'
- *Paul Ingle, probably
Scarborough's best-ever boxer*

Round 7

☐

Hunting with the Big Boys

STRAIGHT after the world championships, with almost 200 fights behind me I was ready to permanently ditch the headguard.

Despite my record, when I announced to the press that I was turning pro, they were doubtful whether I'd be able to make it in the paid ranks. A number of other fighters who'd topped their weight divisions – such as Peter Richardson and David Starrie – were receiving most of the media attention and being touted as future world champions.

I was not known for being a massive puncher, which they thought would count against me but it was just the kind of motivation I needed to prove that they had got it all wrong.

Turning pro is more than just getting paid to train and fight. It's about having the right team around you, to help guide you through the snake and crocodile infested waters. It's essential to gradually work your way into the ranks and move up when you are ready.

I'd already seen plenty of good fighters turn pro and then be forced into tough fights very early on just for their managers or promoters. Unfortunately, some of them took a real pasting in their first few bouts and never really recovered. Some retired early, others became journeymen. It's very sad, as many could have genuinely become champions.

Whilst thinking who could train me, Ray Simpson gave me a call. He'd mentioned that a few weeks earlier, whilst at an amateur boxing show in Hull, he'd had been chatting with a pro called Terry Morrill, who was training with Steve Pollard. 'Before he signs with anybody, tell him to have a word with Steve,' Terry said. 'He's been in the business a long time and will tell him the do's and don'ts.'

Ray told me that Steve had the type of personality that suited me perfectly and his gym was exactly how I liked it. Looking out for my best interests he did, though, tell me not to sign anything until it felt right and just listen to what he had to say.

I respected Ray's opinion and soon after met with Steve at the gym above the Rayners pub. At the time, I didn't know a great deal about Steve and with the exception of the Olympics I wasn't on mainstream television, so he didn't know much about me either.

He made us a cup of tea and I explained that I didn't turn pro to be a journeyman, I was in it to win titles. Steve understood my aims and suggested we worked together for a few training sessions and then, if we got on, we could make it a more permanent arrangement. Thankfully we clicked straight away.

With Steve sorted as my trainer, there was still one crucial person missing from my team. In order for me to get fights, but more importantly, against the right boxers at the right time and for the right money, I needed a good promoter.

I'd been handed a list of the best boxing promoters in the UK which included Mickey Duff, Frank Warren, Barry

Hearn and started some conversations about what might be available. One promoter offered me a very generous package which included an all-expenses paid house in London, whereas another would have seen me barely able to buy my weekly shop.

I decided to have a chat about it with Steve and he said, 'Have you spoken to Frank Maloney?' I told him I didn't know who he was. Steve laughed, 'You know – the short bloke who promotes the heavyweight world champion, Lennox Lewis?' I replied, 'Does he manage him? Oh, right. In that case, we should give him a call.'

Steve was also being promoted by Frank as he was still active as a professional boxer. Ten years earlier he'd won the central area featherweight title but, by 1993, he was fighting less and training fighters more. However, when Maloney needed him as a human punchbag for an up-and-coming fighter, Steve would always oblige. Tough as nails, crafty as hell and with 10 times the number of rough tactics than Roberto Duran, Steve was always ready to fight.

Steve made the call and Frank invited us down as his guests to watch the Lennox Lewis-Frank Bruno fight in Cardiff in early October and also kindly put us up in a nice hotel nearby. Frank had seen me box as an amateur but, as opposed to many of the media guys and some promoters who thought I'd struggle, he saw something and believed I could go all the way.

Before diving into business, we watched the five fights on the bill, which included a future opponent of mine, Neil Swain, a first round knockout debut by a Welsh lad called Joe Calzaghe and then the final bout where Lennox retained his heavyweight world title by stopping the hugely popular Bruno in seven rounds.

Straight afterwards, me and Frank discussed how

much I would get paid for the first couple of years for a certain number of fights and mapped out a plan which we all liked. The other bonus was that while all the other promoters insisted I trained where they wanted, he said, 'The main thing is that you train. I'm not so concerned where as long you train and train right.' Money-wise, the other promoters had offered half or even three quarters less, however, I didn't want to look desperate and said I would sleep on it.

The morning after, I was confident with my gut feeling and we shook hands. Frank Maloney was now my manager and promoter.

****

ONE thing I've never varied on is punctuality. Whatever time Steve told me to be there I was, on the dot. On one occasion in those first couple of weeks, Steve was giving somebody a right ticking off about being late and started referring to me.

He said to this other lad, pointing to me, 'Do you know what the most impressive thing about him is? I never need to wear a watch when he's around. If I ask him to walk through that door at 1.30pm tomorrow; when he walks in, I know it will be bang on 1.30pm.'

Within no time at all, I felt at home. The gym itself was down Hessle Road, above one of Hull's oldest pubs which looked like it had seen better days. There were only four punchbags, a tiny bit of space to do floor work and it stunk. In all honesty it was a real shithole – but as boxers, we couldn't get enough of it. I didn't want a big posh gym where if I spat on the floor I'd get kicked out. I had a job to do – train and train hard and this place was perfect to ensure that happened.

I soon realised that making the 100 miles round-trip

trek from Scarborough to Hull five days a week in my Ford Fiesta XR2i was going to cost me a fortune. Thankfully I managed to get a local sponsor, Stuart Walker, to cover my costs and that took the worry off my mind.

Within no time, I started to bond really well with the other pro boxers there – Tony Foster, Terry Morrill, Chris Hooper, Darren Christie, Peter Richardson and Steve's son, Sonny. Little did I know how dear a friend Sonny would turn out to be 20 years later.

It didn't take the lads long to make me feel like one of their crew. When I first started sparring, my ears used to stick out of the headguard, so they started calling me 'wing nut'. Eventually I ended up taping my ears to the inside of it.

Steve did a great job in the early weeks helping me lose my amateur boxing bounciness, which I'd previously used to get in and out of my opponent's reach to bag points. Steve's theory was once you've gone in and committed to throwing a punch, why would you want to get out – especially if you've hurt them.

Also, the higher you are in the air, the less power you have so he wanted me to plant my feet more, slow things down a bit and work on generating more power.

In addition, he had me working on angling myself differently in front of my opponent so that I had less of a target on show and coming off at new angles after landing shots. It all made sense and made me realise there was a lot to do before I could even think about titles at that point.

One thing Steve noticed in those early days was my workrate. His initial reaction was that he wanted to not only slow my bouncing around, which I was fine with, but he also wanted to slow down my workrate – which I was not in complete agreement about.

He said, 'Paul, I'm a fitness fanatic myself but you'll

be doing four, six, eight and eventually 12 rounds, so you'll need to last the distance. You have a bit more time now, so pick your shots and get something behind them.'

I didn't totally buy in to Steve's plan, though. My argument was that the people who were operating in my division at world level were all rapid fire but some struggled to keep that pace going over the rounds and provide the crowds with entertainment. I wanted to be the guy that the crowds wanted to look at. I wanted to be an exciting fighter.

After a couple of months, I think Steve was genuinely blown away with the level of fitness I maintained. We'd work for about eight or 10 rounds and he'd ask if I was ok. I'd always say, 'I feel good mate, let's keep going.'

One time he took out the heart rate monitor to check my recovery pulse, looked at the result, gave it a tap to make sure it was working and then said, 'It can't be right it says 39 beats per minute.'

He asked again if I felt ok, checked my blood pressure a couple of times and then soon came to the conclusion that I might just be able to handle that energy level for more than a few rounds.

I was never going to be a concussive puncher but within my first few months training as a pro, I became a very solid one. Steve knew I loved to throw the left hook, so his theory was chuck in another 100 punches on top of that and my opponents will have no chance. It turned out to be the winning formula.

****

BY January 1994, I'd settled down nicely as a professional in training and started to knuckle down for my debut. I'd been fighting at flyweight as an amateur but moved up to bantamweight against my first opponent, Darren Noble, which was scheduled for six rounds on the 23 March.

The nerves were even more immense than normal. I was at the Star Leisure Centre in Cardiff with an impressive card of fighters including the likes of Dennis Andries, Sky Sports filming live and family and friends in attendance. To top it off, the week before, the press had been saying that I lacked punch power and my style was too busy for the pros. I kept wondering if it would come together or I'd crumble.

The number of fans who made the journey from Scarborough was incredible. My mum had organised four coaches and that's not to mention the rest who travelled on their own by car and train. I couldn't fault my fans all through my amateur boxing career, but I was genuinely blown away with the number of people who turned up that night.

The price of the tickets for pro bouts meant it was far more expensive than when they supported me as an amateur. I felt like I owed it to them to win, to make sure it hadn't been a wasted journey.

Darren Noble was pretty much a novice, having only fought once a few months earlier, winning a points decision over four rounds. From the first bell, he was trying to draw me in but my punching was too accurate and my movement made it hard for him to catch me with anything. Although I was still fighting with a certain amount of amateur bounce, I managed to take him out with a crunching hook to the body in the third.

I instantly felt relief on a number of levels. I hadn't let my fans down, the media had something good to take away and I came away without injury.

Five weeks later, I travelled down to the famous York Hall in Bethnal Green and took on Graham McGrath over four rounds. Graham was a journeyman who'd fought 26 times by that stage and had a really awkward style which wasn't ideal in terms of trying to put on a show for the fans.

Steve told me to pepper in and out with punches and not to stand toe to toe, as not only could I get caught but I could pick up a cut unnecessarily. I did exactly as he told me. Although it took me a couple of rounds to get to grips with McGrath's style, I still managed to win on points. However, as a fighter trying to establish himself, it was a messy bout and didn't grab the media's attention.

Four weeks later I was fighting against Neil Swain in Bristol and it turned out to be more of a stinker than my previous match. I'd moved up a weight division again and was now fighting at super-bantam, which I felt far more comfortable with. When I saw Neil at the press conference and weigh-in, he looked skinny and weak.

I thought to myself that I'd blow him away in a couple of rounds. Yet, on the day of the fight he looked massive. He'd obviously taken on his fluids and had a good meal in between and from the moment the bell rang, he came straight for me from his long rangy southpaw stance hitting me with some straight rights. I know he didn't have anything in his glove, but it felt like his hands were 100 kg weights.

In the second round he hit me with a long swinging right hand that stunned me and forced me to go on one knee and take the eight count. Swain came flying at me the second the count was over, but I managed to hold on and keep out of harm's way until the bell.

When I got back to the corner, Steve said, 'Keep your hands up.' I nodded and told him, 'It was a good shot but I'm alright now.' He reinforced the message, 'Work to the body and keep those fucking hands up.'

By round four, it was becoming a bit of a tear up but

I managed to land a great body shot which put him on the canvas and kept him on it. When it landed, he started complaining that I'd hit him below the belt. I turned to him and started shouting in a rage, 'Get up. It was nowhere near, you daft lad.'

I was happy with the result, but not so with the way Neil was acting and also the booing from the crowd. I turned to Steve and asked, 'What's their problem?' Steve ushered me quickly out of the ring, saying, 'Let's get you showered and head back to Scarborough....now.'

The day after, I watched the fight back and replayed the decisive punch in slow motion. As I saw it land, I was wincing. It was bang on the crown jewels and if it had been any lower I would have taken one of his knee caps out.

The ref also thought it was a body blow but, in all honesty, if he would have seen what actually happened, I should have been disqualified. Neil went on to become Commonwealth super bantamweight champion and was always a gent when I saw him at future contests.

The Swain body shot wasn't the only bit of luck I had. A few days later, I was flying down Seamer Road in Scarborough in my car which had a sticker at the back saying, 'Don't let it pass you by'. I used to drive past everyone far too quickly and even used to park it up at speed thinking I was a stunt driver.

On this occasion, I had my mate Daz in the car and I was going so fast I couldn't slow it down before the traffic lights, so went straight through at red and carried on accelerating. Next thing, a police car appeared behind me, overtook us then boxed me in down Valley Road.

Two policemen walked over and one tapped on my window and asked me to get out of the car. I stepped out and before he could say anything, I shook his hand and told him

The Yorkshire Hunter

I was so relieved it was the police, because I thought it was a crazed fan chasing me.

The policeman knew who I was, smiled and said, reassuringly, 'No worries, Paul. You drive home safely. No crazy fans around here.' I looked relieved, 'There are some crazy stalkers out there, you know,' I told him. 'I know, drive carefully,' he replied. When I got back in the car, Daz was sitting there with his mouth open wide in amazement.

Before the end of the year, I managed to bag two more points victories over Anthony Hanna and a rematch with Graham McGrath to end the year 5-0. I started 1995 in a similar way, winning two contests back-to-back against the same opponent, Peter Buckley.

Peter is a boxing gentleman. He later retired having fought 300 times as a professional. After my second victory against him, I still wasn't satisfied with my form. I remember Frank Maloney saying, 'It won't be long before you're ready for a 10-rounder with the way you're going.'

Although I was happy that I was undefeated, I wasn't content with the fact that I'd been involved in some scrappy bouts; five of which I'd won on points, one by an illegal low blow and the other on a legitimate knockout.

I looked ordinary and the media pretty much said that. Those watching on television wanted to see me knocking people out or stopping them and I was conscious I hadn't been doing that.

A couple of days after the Buckley rematch, I decided I needed a relaxing break and spoke to my good mates Wayne Smith and Neil Cox about a lads holiday. We went down to the travel agents and booked a week in Turkey for six of us in all. The only thing was, me and Wayne were absolutely skint and, as the holiday date got closer, we started to panic a little about how we would survive out there. I wasn't on big purses yet and Wayne had just come out of the army and was looking for work.

Whilst stressing out about the lack of cashflow, we decided to walk into town and stretch our legs. As we passed the post office, I asked him how much cash he had on him. He told me about a fiver and I persuaded him that we should get some scratch cards and go halves on any winnings.

We won about four quid back from the first lot and agreed to reinvest but instead of scratching them off there and then, we took them back to my mum's house.

We were in the front garden scratching away when Wayne suddenly started jumping and shouting, 'Get in there, we've won a grand!' and passed me the card which had three £1,000 symbols showing. Soon we were both screaming, leaping up and down on the front lawn hugging each other. When mum came out and asked what all the commotion was, we told her and she had a bit of a scream herself.

With our spending money sorted, we headed off to Turkey and had a real laugh. We'd go out for a few beers every night, but the lads were respectful that I was a pro boxer, apart from one evening.

I hadn't eaten a big dinner because I was still aware of keeping on top of my weight and after the first couple of pints was pretty much drunk. Neil Cox handed me a pint and it slipped straight through my hands, hit the ground and the glass shattered into pieces.

Everybody around the bar started clapping whilst I was trying to play it cool as if nothing had happened. Less than a minute later, Coxy ordered me another and exactly the same thing happened again.

We decided to make a swift exit and, as were walking to the next drinking hole, I suddenly realised the lads had disappeared. I'm not sure how I lost the pack but I started panicking a bit as my sense of direction isn't great and started going from one bar to the next looking for them.

The more I looked for them, the more annoyed I became and my last hope before attempting to find my way home was the Temple nightclub, which we'd hit a few nights before. It was a massive place with a balcony overlooking a packed dance floor and hundreds of people bopping away.

As I walked in, I spotted them straight away and made a beeline through the crowd at rapid speed waving my fist above my head and shouting all kinds of insults at them. I was like Moses crossing the Red Sea, as hundreds of clubbers split to the left and right to let the madman walk through.

I ran up the stairs fuming but they couldn't stop laughing and the angrier I became, the more they laughed. In the end I stopped and looked at them and within seconds we were all in fits.

****

THE holiday served its purpose well. I came back re-energised and feeling extremely positive. A few days after arriving back in Scarborough, I was straight back over to Hull and into a training camp for a fight against Des Gargano.

Although Des was another journeyman who had lost 107 bouts, he also had over 30 wins and more tricks up his sleeve than Paul Daniels and Dynamo combined. The first round, he tried everything to break my rhythm, get me out of range and distract me.

As I was about to throw a punch, he'd look at the ring apron, start talking to people in the crowd, or point to something randomly to make me lose my concentration and leave me open for a sucker punch. I realised that I didn't want to be in the ring with this guy too long, as it would be a matter of time before I was caught with one of his illusions.

Thankfully, I managed to stop him in round two and felt fantastic as I'd been desperate to get a stoppage. Apart from one championship fight further down the line, none of my fights would last the distance from this point on.

My fourth fight of 1995 was against Miguel Matthews who I stopped in four rounds without too much bother. He was totally different to Gargano who was constantly in your face – Matthews was always on the back foot which meant I had to be cautious and not get over eager moving forward.

For my last encounter that year, I faced a Bulgarian called Demir Nanev. I knocked him out in the fifth and felt I was getting some momentum.

Steve Pollard was making sure he was keeping fit, too, as he took on my old mate Peter Richardson, who was unbeaten and saw the clash as a stepping stone for a title match. Although Peter beat him up for eight rounds, he came out with a few lumps and bumps and his hands were totally blown up.

After the fight he told me, 'It was a bit strange fighting your trainer. Steve is a tough fella. I kept hitting him and he just wouldn't go down. He kept coming at me like a madman.'

With my progress, I ended my involvement in one of Scarborough's biggest sporting annual events, the Scarborough Coal Hump. It started in 1975 and was well-known as one of the toughest endurance events. In a team of four people, you had to run with a sack of coal weighing four stone over four-and-a-half miles. My good mates and sparring partners George Rhodes and Mark Legge had been taking part for years and set a course record of just over 27 minutes.

The Yorkshire Hunter

In 1991, I joined the team with them and a top man called John Raw and we represented Scarborough Boxing Club. Mark and George had been champions for seven years and had even set a world record on one occasion, with Norris McWhirter timing them for the *Guinness Book of Records*.

I'd never done it before, but the expectations were high. The first time I did a practise run I was really surprised with how difficult it was. When you have a sack of coal on your back it crushes your lungs and makes it more difficult to breath.

Come race day, there were some massive guys in the other teams who were about twice the size and five times as strong. When they looked over at us, they laughed.

We'd worked out that running ability and lung capacity was the key to this, not brute strength. We'd also got our changeover down to a fine art to give us the edge. If I had the sack, then two of the other lads would go either side of me, lift the sack off my back, and the fourth member of the group would go underneath. We'd then gently drop it on his shoulders and he would start running. If you dropped it on the floor, you could lose a minute trying to pick it up and regain the momentum.

The race started by the railway station, then headed off towards Cayton Bay and out towards Seamer. Routes would change each year but the distance was always the same. We completed the course in just over 26 minutes and broke the record.

Having taken part for four years and with title shots possibly on the horizon, I just couldn't risk getting an injury so 1995 was my last go. My back had always caused me some problems and it became clear that it was going to get worse. I'd been a pro for almost two years, was still unbeaten and had begun to interest the media a little more because of the three consecutive stoppages. I was stronger, faster and more determined than I'd ever been and Frank Maloney was fuelling my hunger by keeping me nice and busy.

On the 5th February 1996, he put me in for my first ten-rounder against Greg Upton who had won the Western Area super featherweight title. He was set to be my first proper test.

I felt in great shape throughout the training camp leading up to it and knew in my heart I could take him. I sparred more and ran a bit further, adding in some explosive sprints.

Although Greg was a very durable kid, with just over a minute to go in the final round I threw a left hook to the body followed by one to the head and stopped him. One thing I did notice afterwards was that my hands were killing me with the volume of punches I'd landed.

Although my next two fights against Ervine Blake and Brian Robb were scheduled for eight rounds, I knocked them both out in the second before taking out Chris Jickells, who'd won the Central Area featherweight title about six months previously in four. It made a few more sit up and take notice.

That was a strange night, though, as Steve Pollard was fighting on the undercard. Although stopped in the sixth, he was still in good enough shape to see me through my win.

I'd been on a sensible learning curve. My opponents had been handpicked by Frank Maloney and each served a purpose to see how I was moving in the ring and reacting to power and speed. I must have been doing well because the stakes were about to rise – significantly.

'**H**e had that eye of the
tiger. He was really up
for it, as if it was a
world title shot. That's when I
said to myself, 'You've got a
hard fight here."
- *Colin McMillan, former world
featherweight champion*

Round 8

□

Stepping Up

THE opportunity to fight Colin McMillan had come up about a year earlier and with short notice. Although I was confident in my ability in 1996, after a lengthy discussion with Steve Pollard, we decided to have a few more fights first and not take the risk of putting my career back a couple of years.

Now the time was right. Within 24 hours of the Jickells fight, Frank Maloney was busy getting the contest together which, in all honesty, wasn't too difficult for him because he also had Colin under contract and agreed the bout would be on his home turf in east London.

Colin was certainly not a spent force and I had a lot of respect for what he had achieved. If I won against somebody with his record, I knew it would pave the way for a future world title shot.

As I told Steve, 'I've never been so ready for any fight in my life.'

I had eight weeks to get my body and head into the best shape I'd ever been. Normally I'd have wanted a 10-week training camp but this was the opportunity of a lifetime.

The Yorkshire Hunter

The preparation went fantastically. Steve had a big pub at the time called Ringside with a gym above it. In addition to putting in the hard graft, we watched a number of Colin's old fights on video cassette. We viewed them so many times and had gone through the game plan in training over and over again, that we nearly wore them out.

It became obvious that Colin was a very smooth boxer. We decided we needed to rattle him, rough him up early and overwhelm him with punches.

Steve had calculated Colin's average punch rate over a number of fights and we decided I would throw more, in fact, double. Steve had clocked me averaging 280 punches in three minutes on the bag. The highest I ever did was 328 and if I managed to throw half that amount in a round, it would be suffocating. It wasn't about power and technique but purely workrate.

In addition to the videos I upped the length of my runs, put in more sprint work for the bursts I would expect during the fight and also had a great nutritionist in Joe Dunbar, to advise with the correct foods and supplements, before, during and after training.

I also had my secret weapon, Kenny Brocklehurst or 'Brock'. I'd known Kenny since we were kids growing up on the Edgehill estate and we'd spent many years together fishing, ferreting and shooting. We were both on the table tennis team at the local youth club and won quite a few trophies.

What made Kenny essential to me was his boxing knowledge. From an early age he loved the sport, not just watching all that came on television, but also devouring *Boxing News* and any boxing encyclopaedias from cover to cover, memorising every little statistic and story.

With the exception of the overseas fights, he attended

all of my amateur bouts and once I went professional he never missed a single one. He'd always come to my training camps and stay at dingy bed and breakfasts near the fight venues, even if it meant skipping work to do so.

The team I had around me for the McMillan fight worked really well. It wasn't like some of these boxers you see on TV who have a person to comb their hair, one to tie their shoelaces and another to produce a tissue in case they sneeze. It was a small group with little or no distractions, no circus, just boxing and tons of focus. I went into that fight full of confidence.

We had five sparring partners in the weeks leading up to it and none of them could keep up with my punch rate or power. However, sparring partners were not Colin McMillan, they don't tend to be former world champions.

I was also aware that I'd only fought once in a ten-rounder and this was my first 12-round bout. Indeed, I'd only clocked up ten rounds in total in my last three fights. I was keeping realistic and using such thoughts to keep me sharp.

The Royal Oak gym was about a quarter of a mile from the ramshackle bed and breakfast we were staying at in Canning Town, so we decided the day before the fight to stretch our legs and drop in and say hello to the legendary trainer and manager Terry Lawless, who was a friend of Steve Pollard's.

On the way out, we saw a bookies and decided to pop in. Steve asked the lad behind the desk the odds for the fight and he replied, 'Three-to-one on Colin McMillan and 9-2 for Paul Ingle to win.' Steve, with no fuss, then pulled out a grand and put it on me. The bookie was stunned and in his strong east London accent said, 'What the fuck do you know that we don't know?'

Steve turned to me, looked back at the bookie and

pointed. 'That's Paul Ingle.' He seemed astonished, eyed me up and said, 'He won't beat McMillan,' so Steve asked him for better odds, without success.

****

IT dawned on me at the weigh-in just how many people had come to support me. It was like mini Scarborough. Without a doubt, this was the biggest turnout I'd ever had and the noise they made was crazy.

When I was an amateur, my friends and family were not always able to come and watch me, especially my friends, because they simply didn't have the cash to follow me all around the UK.

However, by 1997, most of my mates were on salaries and pretty much none of them missed a fight. Same goes with my immediate fans in Edgehill and Scarborough. I couldn't fault them and knew that if I won, they won – and so did many pub landlords.

By now, they'd become pretty close with the manager at the Dundee Arms pub as I'd already fought five times at York Hall and he'd have some great banter with them. He had no doubt the London boy would win, though.

The night of the fight, the television crew placed a camera to roll non-stop in the changing room. Steve Pollard looked at them and said, 'You don't want to do that if you are thinking about airing more than 30 seconds.'

Not long after one of them returned and said, 'We can't air that. I've never heard anybody swear so much in such a short space of time. We counted over 1,000 swear words in just under two hours.'

In the last 20 minutes before ring entrance, the respective fans were shouting the house down. I had to pop my Walkman on to help drown out the noise and get some focus. I'd never experienced anything like this.

As I made my way to the ring, I was so focused, spitting and growling. As impressive as Colin's fans were, mine were 10 times louder.

From the opening bell Colin was very smooth, gliding around the ring, firing off hooks whilst moving off at angles. He wasn't called 'Sweet C' for nothing. But by the end of round three I felt that I was ahead. The computer had picked up that he had landed eight body shots, whereas I had hit with 35 and I'd been throwing over 100 punches per round.

In round four I managed to get the edge I needed by opening a cut over Colin's eye with a sharp hook. From that moment on, I wanted to work on it and was trying to get Colin to drop his guard so I could get a clean shot to his head.

The plan was to throw the hook to the body so he would drop his elbow to cover up his ribs and a split second later I'd throw the hook to the head again. It worked. Colin came back firing a number of shots but nothing that worried me.

For the referee it was an easy night as neither one of us wanted to hold on as we threw and countered right up to the final bell.

Come round five, I took control and at one point had Colin on the ropes and must have thrown about 50 unanswered punches. I landed 19 body punches in that round whereas Colin threw none. I'm sure that everybody watching must thought I'd blown my engine but by the time the bell sounded for round six I was on fire again.

Fair play to Colin, he came out all guns blazing for the sixth and although he tagged me with some good shots during the round, I could tell he was starting to get a bit demoralised with me not getting tired or slowing down.

The Yorkshire Hunter

As I came back to my corner at the end of the round, Steve told me, 'His combinations are slowing down and he looks like he needs a breather. Make him work, when he doesn't want to work.'

First minute of round eight, we both traded punches in the centre of the ring but, as we approached the halfway mark, I could sense the bounce had gone from Colin's step. Where he had been throwing threes and fours before, he was unloading single shots without any power, so when the opportunity came, I jumped straight in.

After about 20 punches nonstop to the head and body, I threw a massive left uppercut straight through the middle, which almost took Colin's head off and then followed it with a jab and straight right cross.

Colin fell in a heap between the bottom two ropes and was bleeding pretty heavily all over his face. Thankfully the referee didn't even start the count and waved over the doctors.

I was one of the few people to ever stop Colin. In fact, I was probably the only one to stop him legitimately as his other two were the result of a cut eye and a damaged shoulder.

As the referee waved the fight off, I sprinted over to the side of the ring where my fans were and put my arms up screaming in joy. It was like Scarborough in London. The support was tremendous, but one man caught my eye in particular.

Kevin Cowley, the guy who'd bought me my amateur gear when I was 14, was standing ringside screaming and shouting in joy. As he tried to extend his arm out to congratulate me, two bouncers suddenly appeared in front of him and grabbed an arm each and were going to kick him out.

Even with all the mayhem in the crowd, Colin still lying down on the canvas, Steve and my corner hugging me and the buzz of having just become British champion, I still managed to stick my head through the ropes and shout to them, 'Oi, leave him alone – that's my dad.' The bouncers looked over at me, apologised and let him go. I gave Kev a wink and he was laughing his head off.

I rushed straight back over to Colin and checked he was ok and thanked him for the opportunity to fight him. He would later tell the press that he'd underestimated me a bit. 'I'd fought guys who were bigger and stronger than Paul and who at that point had proved themselves to be better boxers as professionals. He really surprised me. Paul Ingle is a tremendous fighter with a terrific work rate and I'm sure will go far in the sport.'

It was a real honour to hear words like that from a great boxer.

Colin retired after that fight. He had an incredible career, was a world champion and I will always be very grateful for the chance he gave me. He is a total gentleman and the amount he does for charity is outstanding. Little did I know he would be helping me out a few years later.

The second we got back to the dressing room, Steve told me that was my best performance to date. After I'd retired years later, he'd still maintain it was my greatest-ever fight. He told me, 'You never once took your foot off the gas, never once took a backward step and you listened to everything I told you. I'm very proud of you.' I felt on top of the world.

Frank Maloney was equally chuffed as I was his second Olympian who he'd taken up to a title fight. In fact, he was so delighted that he had hired out a pub down the road from his offices in Petticoat Lane for a party.

I had a few drinks, but was also aware of my limits. Steve on the other hand, along with Maloney and a packed pub, partied hard. Frank kept the champagne flowing like water. God knows what the bar bill must have been at the end of the night.

****

A FEW days after the McMillan fight, my good mate Neil Cox asked me if I fancied going on holiday with him. He suggested a nice relaxing week in Tenerife. Having just won the British title, I had a few quid in my pocket and felt like I deserved a treat, so I said why not.

Those were the days when you would either look for a holiday on Teletext, or you would walk to your local travel agent to find out what deals were on. Neil tried both but rang to say he'd got us on a cheap flight from Birmingham and, because he knew a few of the hotel owners there, would fix us up a room when we landed. I wasn't so sure but he'd always come up trumps so went along with it.

We landed at 8pm and, after a long day's travel, I just wanted a nice meal, a cold beer and a long sleep before waking up to sunbathe on a nice sandy beach.

We arrived in Playa de las Americas and Neil confidently marched into the first four-star hotel to ask for a room only to find it fully booked. This routine went on for about the next 15 hotels by which time it was two in the morning and we were both walking the streets deflated.

Next thing there was a power cut which meant all the partygoers spilled out of all the bars and clubs trying to get us to dance and, to top it off, a massive thunderstorm started. I stood there with my leather suitcase over my head as the rain came down like it was the end of the world.

In the end, we found a restaurant doorway and slept inside it with our arms wrapped around our luggage so that nobody could pinch it. I'm surprised we didn't wake up covered in coins, because we looked like a couple of homeless persons.

A few hours later we went to a place where they hired out cars and rented apartments. We hired a car firstly, because if we couldn't find a room, at least we'd have something to sleep in. Thankfully the guy found us a great three-bedroom apartment in Los Cristianos for only £140 for the whole week.

We had fallen on our feet and the rest of the holiday was fantastic. We even bumped into light heavyweight boxer Crawford Ashley who was in training for the European title.

****

ON my return to the UK, I was genuinely knocked back by the support from everybody, especially a local car dealership.

As much as I liked to cruise around in my clapped out Fiesta, I simply couldn't turn down the chance of a brand new sponsored car.

Soon after the McMillan fight, Jordans called and asked if I was interested in a vehicle for a year. I turned up not expecting much but in under a couple of minutes I was handed the keys to a brand new sporty 220 Rover and on the front it said, 'Paul Ingle – British featherweight champion. Sponsored by Jordans.' I couldn't believe it.

It was the first new car I'd ever had. The smell and zero mileage on the clock was fantastic, but feeling appreciated meant a lot more. We did a photo shoot for the press and I told them how humbled I felt and that I'd take really good care of it.

About a week after getting the car, my girlfriend

drove me into town and whilst pulling away at the roundabout, she hit the accelerator, clipped the kerb and flipped the car. She'd only passed her test a short while before and the car was just too powerful for her. She was bruised but thankfully was ok. The car however was a write-off.

I walked back in to Jordans the day after and told them about the accident. They then let me know she wasn't insured. Without any fuss, though, they added her and gave me a new car. As I walked out, I said, 'I'm really sorry. Although it might not look like it, I'm very appreciative of the car. There won't be any more mess ups.'

A few weeks later, I took the new car back because there was a light flashing on the dashboard and I wanted them to take a look. As I walked in, the showroom manager asked, very politely, if he could have a word with me in his office.

I thought to myself that, maybe, it was an upgrade. Once we were seated and the door was firmly closed, he said, 'You know the tickets you keep getting on your windscreen, there's about £1,000 of fines to be paid.'

I was astonished and told him that I've never received anything through the post.

He replied, 'You wouldn't as all fines are sent to the showroom address where the car is registered. I'd be very appreciative if you could start to watch where you park.'

I was very apologetic and embarrassed.

Three months after the McMillan fight, I was back in action against Michael Alldis to defend my British title at the Ice Arena, Hull. It was the biggest venue I'd fought at and it was like a homecoming.

'Team Ingle' certainly made their mark that night and that was before the first bell had rung. Frank Maloney caused ructions because he had the most scantily dressed ringcard girls ever. We were asked by a senior official from the British Boxing Board of Control to bar them from the ring.

Fair play to the mayor of Scarborough, Sheila Kettlewell, who was a big fan of boxing and a loyal supporter of my fights. She turned to the official and said, 'I'm not offended by it. It's all part of promoting the show.' That was that. The official walked off with a face like a sack of spanners.

As Steve Pollard was stepping through the ropes, he nicked the top of his head on one of the bolts of the metal framework in the corner. Mick Williamson turned to him and said, 'Unbelievable Pollard, the first cut of the night I have to attend to isn't even one of the fighters.' We were all laughing.

I'd seen Michael in action as an amateur. He was very fit and strong but he was naturally a super bantamweight who tended to work at one pace and couldn't go through the gears. That night I was able to hit him pretty much at will and stopped him in the 11th.

Many other fighters wouldn't have lasted as long as he did. Michael went on to become the British and Commonwealth super bantamweight champion and won the Lonsdale belt.

A few days later, I went on holiday to Tenerife again but with five mates this time. Halfway through the week, we went to a massive bar called Veronicas as they were showing the Prince Naseem Hamed versus Billy Hardy fight.

Billy was challenging Naz for his IBF and WBO world featherweight titles but unfortunately didn't make it out of second gear as Naz stopped him in the first round.

In the meantime, whilst I was trying to keep a low profile, one of my mates decided it would be nice to go up to the DJ and get him to shout out, 'We have a special guest this evening, the British featherweight champion, Paaaaaul

Innnnngle. Put your hands together for the champ – he's standing over there.'

Everybody was clapping and going crazy, wanting photos and autographs. I was fuming and wanted to get out of there straight away.

A few days later, I was back in Scarborough and jumped straight into full-time training getting ready to fight the featherweight Commonwealth champion, Jon Jo Irwin. I'd also be putting my British title on the line for a winner-takes-all belt contest.

I'd sparred Jon Jo as an amateur and he was an excellent fighter who became the English captain. He looked like a throwback from the 1970s with a big mop of hair and the long, thick sideburns and, in my opinion, was too nice a person to be a boxer.

However, the fight almost didn't happen because I failed a drugs test. I'd hurt my ankle about a week before and was desperate to get the fluid off it, so took a diuretic tablet which helped to reduce the fluid but unfortunately didn't do my urine sample any favours.

I had to go up in front of the British Boxing Board of Control in London but, thankfully, Frank Maloney helped me through the process. He asked Joe Dunbar, who was not only my nutritionist but had also worked with Lennox Lewis and a number of other world class athletes, to go over my drug report in detail.

In the end, Joe was able to prove that I'd taken a diuretic to reduce ankle swelling but at no point had I taken any performance-enhancing drugs. He managed to get me off without any penalties, banning, or even worse, having my British title taken away.

I did, however, come away with a slapped wrist and had to pay far more attention to the way I trained and what

I consumed. The whole experience was a rude awakening, but thankfully the Irwin fight was still on.

We had very similar boxing styles but the main difference was his three-inch height advantage, so the plan was to go to work on his body and wear him down.

As with the McMillan fight, the training camp went very well. We'd got all the videos, studied him in detail and everything went to plan. The only hiccup was that for some unknown reason, the fight didn't start until 1.30am. We never did find out why either.

There was a point as we were hanging around when Steve turned to me and said, 'The television crews have gone home and it sounds like they are packing up outside. I don't think you're going to fight tonight.' I was devastated and mad all at once.

The delay also caused a real problem for the fans, many of whom had parked up in car parks which closed at midnight and either went home or had to find another place. My mum had organised about five coaches of fans who'd travelled up from Scarborough and she had to ask the drivers to stay longer and in the end pay them extra to hang around. It was the kind of hassle any fighter could do without, especially so close to a fight.

Eventually, it did happen and my best memory of the evening was stopping Jon Jo in round eight to become the new Commonwealth champion. My strangest memory however, was fighting whilst hearing the sound of scaffolding being taken down throughout the fight as they were dismantling the seating. By the end, the hall was pretty much empty.

In addition, I'd won the Lonsdale belt. This was the one I had wanted since my amateur days and I used to say to my mum, 'I'm going to get one of those for you one day.' The moment I received it, I handed it over. Even now, whenever I take the belt out of my cabinet at home she says, 'You can borrow it if you want.'

My first test of 1998 was a defence of my Commonwealth belt against Trust Ndlovu, in Hull in March. I wouldn't say it was a walk in the park but by using my speed and distance I was able to beat him 120-109. It was a good learning experience as I went 12 rounds for the first time, but he was never a threat.

Less than three months later, I was up against Moussa Sangare, who had unsuccessfully challenged Manuel Medina for his world crown a few years before, losing a close majority decision. I managed to go one better by retiring Moussa in ten rounds, which certainly got the sanctioning bodies' attention, as I was now rated in the world top ten by the WBC, WBA and IBF.

The second half of the year was a defining period of my career. Less than two months after the Moussa fight, I was up against the Ukrainian super featherweight champion Rakhim Minhalieyev, fighting for the IBF featherweight Intercontinental title.

Frank Maloney had finally made the dream come true, he organised the fight to happen at the Spa in Scarborough. It had been great appearing in Hull for my last two fights, the support was immense, but ever since I turned pro, I couldn't wait to fight in my beloved Scarborough.

Maloney said, to me, 'Scarborough doesn't have a great football team at the moment and is probably known for hosting conferences and short breaks. I want you to be marketed as Scarborough's premier sporting star and get the community to follow.'

Marketing myself certainly wasn't my bag, but I kind of understood what he was saying and left him and Rocky

Rowe to it. I wanted to make sure that what might be my only opportunity to fight at home would be something special for me to cherish for life.

The only problem was that the Spa only had one slot available and that was in August which was not ideal as I'd just come off fighting 22 rounds and Frank had already organised a big battle with Billy Hardy for the European title the following month.

On the flip side, winning the IBF Intercontinental title would move me up their rankings and get me closer to challenging for the world title.

****

THE build up to the Minhalieyev fight was pure madness. Rocky Rowe is an ex-marine who used to live in Plymouth, running a couple of very rough pubs whilst being involved in the unlicensed boxing scene.

I first met him at a fundraiser in Scarborough which was trying to raise cash to send me to the Olympics. He'd just moved into the area at the time and had bought a pub, nightclub and hotel.

By the time I turned pro, I'd got to know Rocky very well and his generosity towards me was incredible. Not that I ever needed a bodyguard, but he's a big strong man, standing over six-feet tall, about four-feet wide and with a massive personality to match. Whenever we were out, he'd always be keeping an eye on me in the shadows, making sure nobody was trying to be clever with me.

Rocky's part in the Minhalieyev build up was legendary, so much so that people often refer to the parties around it more than the fight itself.

Above Rocky's nightclub, which had four bars

blasting out music until the early hours, he had a hotel and was doing a deal for any of my fans. In fact, everyone in my camp was also staying there, including Frank Maloney and my sparring partners, such as Toncho Tonchev and Patrick Mullings.

Toncho stayed with Rocky for about six months in the end and became like one of the family.

When the rooms were full Rocky would improvise. For this fight, it booked up really quickly and instead of turning the fans away, Rocky put down a load of mattresses in the hallways with a few coffee tables and lamps and also had people sleeping in the dining room.

Quite a few of the guests would end up getting drunk after leaving the bars downstairs, which led to many forgetting to close their room doors. Consequently, when they went to the loo, they would often come back to the wrong room.

On one particular night, this lady walked into the wrong room and jumped into a double bed which three old men were sharing. They all freaked out and came running downstairs, shouting to Rocky's wife about this mad woman who was trying to assault them.

By the time morning came, the hallways in Rocky's hotel looked like army trenches and it carried on for the days, before, during and after the fight. Only Rocky could pull it off.

The weigh-in for this fight was crazy too. Rocky had set up a ring in a big yard behind the nightclub, so I could spar publicly but it was also the perfect place for the media. Frank Maloney was well known for getting his office staff to wear costumes and a few months earlier had made Ed Robinson dress as a devil for the fight between Herol Graham and Vinny Pazienza.

Rocky had a white horse and Maloney had wanted to

bring all his fighters in on it but the officials wouldn't allow it, so he got a lad called John to do it instead. Rocky asked him if he'd ever ridden a horse and he said no. Rocky told him not to worry and to just jump on and he'd be ok. John was obviously petrified.

After Patrick Mullings was getting ready to jump on the scales for his world title challenge against Simon Ramoni, John made his entrance like an uncomfortable Zorro on the big white horse and the photographers started clicking away with their massive flashes. The horse started getting jumpy which then made the lad panic. Within seconds the horse bolted off, throwing John clean off. Nobody was hurt, but the media certainly got value for money.

After buckaroo left the weigh-in, it was time for me to jump on the scales. Normally, Patrick would have been the last to go as he was challenging for a world title, but because this was my homecoming fight, I was made top of the bill.

When I stepped on to the scales I was two pounds overweight and there was a massive sigh from everyone as the media started scribbling away like mad. However, I knew what I was doing and just wanted to add to the entertainment factor.

I was wearing massive Bermuda shorts and started to take out my mobile phone, a set of keys, a handful of coins, another mobile phone, my wallet and finally the Bermudas – with a pair of undies still on – and was bang on the weight. The crowd burst into laughter as I did my striptease and then went crazy as my weight was called out as perfect by the officials.

The fight was a matter-of-fact contest where I just took care of business. I stopped Minhalieyev with a body shot in the fourth and was now the holder of three titles.

The party after the fight went on for two days. Rocky

pulled every string possible to make that show something else – and it was. That fight will stick with me forever; the build-up, the atmosphere and the reception we got.

****

JUST six weeks later, I was fighting in York against Billy Hardy. Billy turned pro at 19 and over his 47 fights at that point had won the British, Commonwealth and European titles in two weight divisions, not to mention three world title shots and winning the Lonsdale belt outright.

Although he was coming to the end of his career, he was certainly one of the toughest opponents I'd come up against at that point. I was placing my Commonwealth belt on the line, whilst he brought the European title to the table and gave me the opportunity to take one step closer to world title recognition.

For no particular reason, on the day of the fight, I decided to go down to the barbers and got my hair spray-painted to match my camouflage shorts. Straight after the paint dried, I put a cap on and kept it on all day, so the media couldn't get a look. When I turned up to the changing room, Steve Pollard was chatting to my cut man and without even taking a breath from his conversation said, 'What the hell have you done to your hair? That paint better not run.'

The fight itself was exciting, as we went toe-to-toe from the off. From the opening bell I felt my timing and movement was bang on and a step ahead of Billy's. That said, he caught me with a left hook in the first couple of rounds which to this day remains the hardest punch I've ever felt.

I managed to wear him down over the next few rounds and in round eight, I threw one of the best single punches I'd thrown in my career. It was a nice straight right hand just over the top of Billy's guard which sent him to the canvas and had the referee waving it off straight after.

Soon after being crowned European champion, I decided to buy my own house. I'd lived with my mum all my life and felt that the time was right to leave the nest. I had a few quid in the bank from my recent title fights, so also decided to splash out on a new car too.

After returning the Rover back to Jordans, much to their relief no doubt, I bought a small BMW from a local dealership. I'd only had the car about nine months when I received a call from the guy at the garage saying, 'You've had that car for a while now. We've got one we think you should test drive. There's no obligation, just come and have a spin and it's up to you.'

I walked into the showroom and saw this immaculate brand new BMW 328i convertible with all the racing kit and I was hooked. I took it for a test drive and it flew. I drove it out of there the same afternoon. Although I said I would never get a personalised number plate, I couldn't resist it and got, 'TKO'. Life was certainly very good.

'**Ladies and gentlemen. Please stay seated and fasten your seatbelts tightly. We have an issue with one of the engines. We are going to be dropping altitude rather quickly, but ask you remain calm at this time as everything is in hand.'**
- *Pilot announcement, en route to New York*

Round 9

□

America Beckons

STRAIGHT after the Hardy fight, Frank Maloney publicly announced to the press that we wanted Naz. I'd won four titles in just over 18 months, climbed up the rankings and was being called out by a number of world class boxers. I even said in an interview with Sky, 'We've always been hunting Naz down. It's finally come. The hunter has caught up with its prey.'

Soon after the Hardy fight, Steve Pollard gave me a call, very excited, shouting down the phone, 'You've got the Naz fight.'

I asked Steve how much the promoter was offering and he said £160,000. I calmly told him, 'Tell him I want £300,000.'

We already had a fight organised in Scarborough against tough former world champion Steve Robinson for £30,000 and I'd also been given another world title opportunity from Don King, to take on the WBA featherweight champion Antonio Cermeno in New York, on the Lewis-Holyfield undercard but, again, the cash was way too low.

Fighting Naz was a different story. Compared to everyone I'd fought and everyone I knew of in the featherweight division, he was a big risk. Steve thought I was being ridiculous and pricing myself out. I was convinced that a match-up between me and Naz would be explosive and full value for money.

Steve called me back and said, 'They've asked me to tell you, either accept the £160k today or the fight's off.' We then went to the press, without disclosing any sums of money, and said that we would likely take the Robinson fight as the offer from Naz's camp was insufficient

At this level, the championship belts and the money are part of a circle, which if you step away from it's tough to jump back in. By the time the Naz fight was being negotiated, I was European champion and would be giving up my belt to take him on – the main thing that was making me money.

If I lost heavily against him, I probably wouldn't get a look-in from any other world champions for a while and would have to prove myself again. In my eyes, I wasn't being greedy, just sensible with my business and my future.

A couple of days later £200,000 was offered and was refused. A few hours after that, Steve called again and said that their final offer was £225,000.

Nobody had ever got that as a featherweight challenger but I knew they wanted this fight badly, so I stuck to my guns. About four days passed and the offer I wanted came in. In fact, including television and a few other bits and pieces, it worked out to be £345,000.

A few hours after the offer had been accepted, Steve came knocking on my door. Before I could say anything, he looked at me with a serious face and said, 'We can beat this guy, we really can. We both know that the cash is important but we wouldn't have accepted all the money in the world to jump in that ring if we didn't think you had a chance. We can beat Naz. I'll call you tomorrow and we will get cracking.' And within a heartbeat he was off again.

We started the training camp about 12 weeks before fight night set for the 10th April, 1999. As with McMillan, we started to look at videos but quickly came to the conclusion that the only thing predictable about Naz in the ring was that he was totally unpredictable.

He was a maverick. I'm pretty sure he went into the ring throwing punches from positions he hadn't even practised before. He was a massive talent with a concussive punch. We knew that if I walked into one, that would be it.

So the plan was, stay close to him and then edge back, so he would fire and I would bob and weave, get underneath him and make him pay. Our thoughts were that if Naz started firing 10 punches and missed with seven or eight, he would get tired and soon stop firing. The intention was for me to take control of the fight from about the fifth round onwards.

****

A FEW weeks into my training camp, Frank Maloney came up with what he thought was a great idea but one which I wasn't over the moon about. He'd always preferred me to be away from the temptations of my backyard and, as the fights became bigger, he wanted that more than ever.

He called me up all excited and said, 'I'm flying you out to the Poconos in the USA, to train at Lennox Lewis camp for a few weeks,' expecting me to be delighted. I could only hear two words – flying and USA. Flying freaked me out and I wanted to train near where I lived. I must have sounded pretty ungrateful as most people would have jumped at the chance.

Unfortunately, the offer was non-negotiable, as HBO were covering the fight and their exposure in the US was huge. Maloney's intention was to get me to mix with the big names out there to raise my profile and also for them to see first-hand what I was capable of. The plan worked well down the line and helped to set up my next big fight on US soil.

A few days later, I was getting ready to leave from Manchester Airport with Steve Pollard, Rocky, my brother Dean, Patrick Mullings and a few others. Similar to the Tenerife holiday a couple of years before, I wanted to keep a low profile whenever I was mixing with the general public, so I kept my head down, made sure none of the lads were wearing any boxing gear to get any attention and after showing the stewardess my boarding pass, made my way to my seat.

Steve Pollard was behind me and the second his pass had been cleared, he shouted out, 'Put your hands together for the British, Commonwealth and European champion – Paul Ingle. He's fighting for the world title in a few weeks.' I could have gladly got off the plane at that point with embarrassment.

It wouldn't have been as bad if I was already sitting down but I was trapped in the aisle, with people putting down their hand luggage in front of me to clap and others were walking over to shake my hand.

By the time we finally made it to our seats, the cabin crew started showering us with champagne. The second my glass was filled, Pollard's arm leant over and he said, 'You won't be needing that. You stick with the orange juice or water, mate. You're in training.'

As we started to make our journey over the Atlantic and were just about to fly over Greenland, I looked over and could see Rocky, who was sitting by the wing, gazing out of the window looking a bit worried about something. He was as white as a sheet and sweat was pouring off him, which was very unlike him.

He called over the stewardess and pointed something out to her on the wing. The stewardess said, 'Don't worry, everything is ok. We have everything under control.'

Seconds later, loud alarms in the cabin started beeping and an announcement was made to put our seatbelts on and chairs upright.

On the row behind us, Rocky turned to the bloke sitting next to him and said, 'Fuck me, that engine has stopped spinning around.'

All of a sudden the plane started to drop at a crazy rate with the nose sticking up. It was like we were doing a giant wheelie. The stewardesses couldn't push the trolleys up the aisles and all the lights above the seats started to flash like someone had won the jackpot on a fruit machine. I guess you could say the situation was pretty serious.

I genuinely thought we were going down. I was shitting myself but doing my best not to show it to anybody. Despite the fact that my brother Dean had never flown before and it also happened to be his birthday, he remained very calm.

He turned and asked me, 'Does this usually happen when you fly, Paul?'

I was trying not to panic him and replied, 'Usually the landing is a bit smoother than this,' while squeezing the arm rest so tight I had no blood left in my hands.

Rocky was screaming out, 'We're all going to die,' whilst Pollard, who by this stage was shit-faced, was turning to the passengers around him and saying, 'I've had a good life,' and started telling them his story.

It didn't help when we took another dip and the

oxygen masks dropped in front of everybody, which really sent us all into a panic. Kids started screaming and crying, swiftly followed by adults and loads of people getting nosebleeds, including my brother, as we were dropping altitude so quickly. The dip even sobered Pollard up.

Then, the captain made an announcement which started with, 'We have a problem....' Rocky interrupted shouting, 'Fuck me, we have a problem alright.' He then walked to the back of the plane where all the catering was and started sticking bottles of water in his jacket.

I asked him what the hell he was doing and he said that if there was an emergency landing and we had to wait to be rescued, he wasn't going thirsty.

The pilot then said, 'We are going to turn back to Shannon Airport in Ireland.' Five minutes later he came back on, 'We are going to land in the Azores and should be there in two hours.'

When the ocean gets closer and the details of ships and the white of the waves become clearer, trust me, that's the longest two hours of your life. I was checking my watch every five minutes.

Finally we started to see the Azores and landed on a military base which looked like it had one of the widest runways in the world. It was a bit bumpy but the second the plane stopped, there was a massive, collective sigh of relief from everyone and then a round of applause.

As we were walking off the plane, Rocky asked the captain, 'How close were we to ditching?' He replied, 'Close enough.'

From the second the plane landed on the runway, we had a fleet of trucks following us. As we stepped off, one of the first things they said to us was not, 'Are you ok?' but there would be absolutely no photos because it was a military base.

If they found out you'd taken a still or video footage, instant arrest was threatened.

In the meantime, our jumbo jet was making the news headlines because they thought we'd gone through the Bermuda Triangle. Nobody knew where we were and apparently the army base had restricted media coverage for security purposes.

The hotel we were put up in was like a prison. It had some neighbouring communities which were full of gangs and we were told they were very dangerous. We were given a curfew of 7pm and then they locked the doors.

You were allowed one phone call and we were given food and hot drinks, but no alcohol. Me and Dean were sharing a room and, the morning after, I met up with the lads and Steve looked awful.

It had nothing to do with the alcohol either. According to him, Rocky made the loudest noise he'd ever heard produced from a human being. 'When he snores, the doors, windows and bed covers shake,' he said.

Just as we were leaving the hotel and heading back to the airport, the police pulled up and stopped our coach. The manager had reported that a number of bills had not been paid and they weren't letting us board the plane until the slate was clean. We all turned and looked at Steve and Rocky who quickly, with their heads down, went and settled up with the manager.

Taking off from the military base was far worse than leaving Manchester. The runway had been built for fighter jets, which only need a short stretch to take off, as opposed to jumbos. As we started to pick up speed, Rocky started to say, 'We're not going to make it. There's not enough road.' After the day before, I didn't think anything could have made me more nervous but his commentary did.

The end of the runway was a sharp cliff drop and as we came off the ground a matter of metres before the end, there was another huge sigh of relief from all the passengers. By the time we reached New York I was almost ready to kiss the ground and arrange a boat back.

After going through passport control and picking up our cases, we were expecting to be mobbed by paparazzi but due to the fact we'd been on an invisible flight and should have arrived about two days earlier, there was nobody there which, in all honesty, I was happy about.

I was knackered and just wanted to have a few hours' sleep and get into my training. Believe it or not, even with all this going on, Prince Naseem Hamed never escaped my mind for a single moment.

Just when I thought I'd got away with the media, Fox News jumped out of nowhere with a television crew and a beautiful lady with a massive microphone. Steve jumped in front, still fuelled on complimentary champagne, and gave them an epic account of our near-death experience.

In the meantime, Rocky managed to sort us out with a limo as the one Frank Maloney had arranged for the original arrival was obviously no longer waiting.

After a three hour drive, we finally arrived at the Poconos training camp in Pennsylvania. When we caught up with Maloney, he was absolutely delighted to see us but also had a mini-drama of his own.

His famous Union Jack suit had gone missing. He was convinced that it had been mislaid during his stopover in New York and was offering a £10,000 reward for it. He even said he was thinking of contacting the FBI and the CIA. In the end, it turned out that he'd left it behind at his local dry cleaners.

Although I moaned about being away from Scarborough, when I got to the Poconos I was blown away. If anything, it was a little too posh for my liking. The dining room looked like it could have catered for 350 people and had a line of tables with absolutely every kind of food you could ever imagine eating.

The rules at the camp were pretty strict but also very sensible. There was a no drinking policy, no training on a Sunday and there was a strict code of conduct how to behave in the gym.

One of the most memorable things that many boxers take away from training at the Poconos is the famous boxing faces you see and my first afternoon there was no exception.

Lennox Lewis was a big reason why Maloney wanted me over there, because he was just about to fight Evander Holyfield to unify the world titles and was receiving a crazy amount of press. This in turn meant that every time somebody from the media came to see Lennox, they also wanted to speak to me and this would happen quite a few times every day.

Maloney said, 'At the moment you are almost invisible out here. When you come over next time, you'll be world champion and this is the start of getting you on their radar.'

Watching Lennox was an eye opener. I had seen the likes of Mike Tyson on television with Cus D'Amato and saw how he trained like a madman – very similar to myself. However, when I saw Lennox and Manny Steward together, they never seemed to be pushing things to the limits in training or spar an excessive number of rounds.

Manny would coach from outside of the ropes whilst Steve was in my face nonstop and while Lennox who had a massive entourage – one to wrap his hands, one to hold his water bottle and so on, I did all that myself. It must have worked for him because Lennox was an excellent champion.

Manny, like Lennox, was a private guy who only spoke when he was spoken to and after he'd finished his job would leave straight away. When I finally got to meet him face to face, I was expecting him to shake my hand and walk off, but I was knocked back with how friendly and warm a person he was.

He started by saying he was a big fan of my fighting style and also said he would love to have the opportunity to train me in the future. He even gave me some tips on how to fight Naz. 'Stay in front of him and constantly put pressure on him. If you give him room or leverage, he'll throw dangerous shots.'

As flattered as I was, I told him I wanted to stick with Steve and I took what he said with a pinch of salt though as he was going to be in Naz's corner on fight night.

****

THE first night we arrived, I headed back to the room early.

Between jet lag and the plane drama, I wanted a few hours of quality sleep before getting stuck into my first workout. Steve insisted on sharing a room with me and Dean after his experience with Rocky, although he didn't give a bad effort himself on the snoring front.

Dean said he fancied joining me for the morning running session. I looked at him like he'd sprouted a second head.

A few hours after we'd got to sleep, there was a knocking on the door.

When I opened it, Patrick Mullings was standing there shivering with a blanket wrapped around him saying,

'Can I sleep on your floor tonight please? It's Rocky. I can't take his snoring anymore. Seriously, it's killing me.'

Come morning, I was up at the crack of dawn and standing above Dean shouting and pulling the mattress from underneath him; he likes a lie-in. About 15 minutes later, me, Dean, Lennox, his crew and a number of other boxers set off on the mountain run.

Halfway up Dean said, 'To hell with this,' and walked back to base. The air was very thin, many found it hard to breathe, but I outran the whole pack and was first back to the breakfast table on each occasion.

After a good feed and a couple of hours rest, I had my first spar against a future world champ, Frankie Toledo. If I wasn't awake following the run, I certainly was after he knocked me down in the first round.

Although I may have been a bit fatigued, the fact is that Frankie was a cut above most of the sparring partners I'd been used to up to that point in my career. The second I hit the canvas he pulled me up, asked if I was ok and then put his arm around me before we carried on for a few more rounds.

We were very respectful of each other but also aware that we could easily be facing one another in the ring for a title match at some point in the future, so we didn't hold back too much. I also sparred with his brother Dave, who was nonstop for every second of each round. It was just what I needed.

After I'd finished sparring with Frankie on the first Saturday out there, and with a deserved day off to look forward to, I sat back with my guys and watched Lennox sparring.

About five minutes in, an American guy with a thick New York-Italian accent made for Rocky. 'Hi. I'm Joe and I have a limousine. With you as my new buddies, I'd like to take you to New York City for a sightseeing tour on your day off,' he said. We agreed.

Rocky got nine people together to come along and first thing Sunday morning we all waited outside. After about 10 minutes, this transit van chugs up blowing out loads of black smoke and Joe said 'Jump on board guys.'

You have to picture five of Lennox's big heavyweight sparring partners, myself, Rocky, Steve Pollard and Dean squeezing in – to top it off, Joe also brought his little son along, who sat up front on Rocky's knee, whilst the rest of us were packed in the back like a rugby scrum.

A four hour drive later we arrive in Times Square. Some of the heavyweight sparring partners wanted to go to the peep shows but we decided to take in the sights.

Heavyweight Jeremy Williams was with us and said he would show us a few places. In the meantime, the van driver gave us his number and said that when we were done to give him a call and we could meet up.

We enquired about going up to the Empire State Building but it was too foggy, so gave it a miss. After having taken in most of the hotspots, we got a bit tired and tried calling Joe but couldn't get through to him.

After a number of calls and a few hours later, we finally got through to him and he said, 'I'm so sorry guys. I really ruined your day. Can I make it up to you and take you to John Gotti's restaurant?'

Gotti was the notorious head of the Gambino crime family in New York City and was in prison at the time. We didn't feel it would be wise to refuse so agreed on checking his place out.

As we walked into this restaurant in The Bronx, there were a few Italian guys sitting there having dinner with the napkins tucked over their shirt collar, tucking into some massive plates of food and red wine and all conversation stopped.

****

UNFORTUNATELY, after about two weeks, I pulled my back. I'm not even sure how but it was enough for us to head back to Scarborough which, in all honesty by that stage, I was ready for. The biggest fight of my life was a matter of weeks away and I was hungrier than I'd ever been – albeit a bit shaken by the American adventure.

'**N**az may have a
Lamborghini and a
Ferrari, but I have two
whippets and a ferret.'
- *Paul Ingle,*
1999 press conference

Round 10

☐

Naz

BACK on UK soil, I started upping my sparring and had the likes of Graham Earl and Toncho Tonchev in the gym with me on a daily basis, with strict instructions not to hold back.

I had also got into a routine of running at 10pm every night, as that was the time I was scheduled to fight Naz. I wanted to leave nothing to chance.

Steve decided it was time to get the press involved, he wanted to get Naz rattled when hearing about the intensity of my camp so set one up specifically for them. He told the press that my mental and physical capacities would be pushed to their limits and Naz simply wouldn't be able to cope with that.

Camp was established about 10 miles away from Scarborough on the moors, at the bottom of a valley, where you couldn't get any phone reception or radio signal. We had a punchbag hanging from a tree and some tins of meat and beans by a rucksack on the floor, making out l was almost living off the land.

Steve was in the Territorial Army and had access to

all the gear, so when the television and radio crews turned up, we were both dressed in camouflage and I was lifting rocks like weights, with Pollard shouting instructions at me. If I wasn't the Yorkshire Hunter before, I certainly was now.

The media crew turned to Steve and said, 'We can't believe you are staying here.'

He replied, 'Yeah – we are here for two weeks. It's a tough training camp and Naz will know about it when he gets in that ring.'

One of the reporters then noted, 'I don't see any tents. Where are you guys sleeping?

Quick as a flash, Steve replied, 'The Yorkshire Hunter doesn't need a tent. We sleep with a blanket wrapped around us and use our rucksacks as pillows.'

As the crews were starting to take off and out of earshot, one of the lads turned to me and asked, 'What is it like to live here for two weeks?'

I replied, 'I don't know. It's only 10 miles from home and I'm running back, see you later.' It was all just for show and a bit of fun, though it certainly helped to sell tickets.

As rough as the moors were, they weren't half as bad as the venue I had organised for Sky Sports to come and film me at a week later. Most Thursday nights I would play snooker with my mate Neil Cox at the local social club and decided it would be a great venue for the feature.

The social club was never the best place in town on a good day, but there had been a fire a few weeks before but I'd been guaranteed it would be looking first class for the television cameras and they would pull out all the stops.

I'd told the production crew to come over around 8pm. When I walked in about 20 minutes early, I couldn't believe what I saw and by this time it was too late to cancel or rearrange as they had travelled from London specifically for me.

Nothing had been painted or decorated, the carpet didn't fit and hadn't been nailed properly on the steep stairs and there were random holes on the floor and walls. It was a death trap.

In contrast, the formal press conference for the fight went far more smoothly and was in a plush hotel. Everybody was expecting sparks to fly between us, especially as I'd been calling out Naz for about a year but also because he had quite a reputation for undermining his opponents and trying to make them feel honoured he'd given them the opportunity to box him. Although Naz got under many people's skin, in my eyes he was always a gentleman and his family were always lovely to me, my mum and brother. Of course there was a bit of banter in the build-up but it never got nasty.

As amateurs I think I was better than him and, in all honesty, if somebody had asked me back then if I thought he would have got a world title shot before me, especially with him being a couple of years younger than me, I would have said no.

His pro game, however, was very different. He was a two-weight champ who, by the age of 25, had already defended his world titles 12 times and at the time was rated as one of the best pound-for-pound fighters on the planet.

We both agreed that it would be a great fight for Yorkshire and Britain. I think the media were actually slightly disappointed that we didn't kick off.

I did manage to get the room laughing at one point though, when one of the journalists asked me how I felt about fighting someone who had a fleet of sports cars and tens of millions in the bank. I replied, 'Naz may have a Lamborghini and a Ferrari, but I have two whippets and a ferret.' The whole room erupted with laughter and even Naz couldn't help but join in and clap his hands.

The Yorkshire Hunter

After the conference, I had a little bit of fun with promoter Barry Hearn. I used to have a £20 note on the end of a piece of fishing wire and dropped it on the ground near his feet. I was standing about 10 feet away, drinking coffee with a big group of my mates shielding me, who knew exactly what I was up to. I saw Barry look down, then check if anybody was looking, before he quickly bent down to pick it up. As his hand got about five inches from the note, I yanked it away and all my mates started clapping and laughing. Barry wasn't happy.

The weigh-in was held at the Rovers Return pub on the set of *Coronation Street* and although it was fictional was fully functional – as I found out when I turned around to see Daz Smith and my other mates holding up a pint. The atmosphere was mad and it felt like the whole of Yorkshire had turned up to support us in Lancashire.

Ring announcer Michael Buffer loved the pub and was a real joker, but it was Junior Jones, who was fighting on the undercard, who made a real impression on me.

He had a terrific presence about him. He didn't speak very much, in fact we didn't exchange a single word, but his look spoke volumes. Although I didn't have a fight lined up with him at that point, we both knew that our paths could potentially cross and, maybe, that's why we kept each other at arm's length.

The legendary Thomas 'The Hitman' Hearns was also fighting on the same bill and when my mate Daz saw him, he was totally star-struck. Unfortunately, he didn't have any paper on him so he asked Hearns to sign a £20 note, which the star man did. I remember Daz saying to me straight after, 'To have something signed by the man who fought Leonard, Hagler and Duran is unbelievable. I'll keep this forever, it's a prized possession.'

Come fight night and he ran out of money, so the Hearns note was sacrificed to get a round of beers in.

****

THE night before the fight I was staying in a really nice hotel in central Manchester and had Kenny Brock and Eugene Maloney on security. Eugene was as mad as a hatter and dressed up in army gear to get into the whole 'Hunter' vibe.

I must say, as crazy as he was, I liked the guy. I first met him soon after the Lewis-Bruno fight in 1995, when he had slept outside Lennox's hotel room and said to me in his thick London accent, 'You know what Paul, one day you're gonna fight for a world title and I'll sleep outside your hotel room.'

He certainly kept his word and pulled up a sofa, setting up camp in front of the door whilst Kenny Brock slept in the corridor and made sure no fans – or indeed anybody – was allowed to enter my room, unless I'd given permission.

The atmosphere on fight night was unbelievable. The contest was billed by some as the 'Featherweight championship of the world of Yorkshire', whilst others said it was a burglar's paradise in Scarborough that night.

I arrived a couple of hours early and couldn't believe the reception I got as I stepped out of my car at the MEN arena. It's probably the best one I ever had. It was as if the whole of Scarborough had turned up and filled the place.

I wasn't able to drive my girlfriend over, so I asked my mate Wayne Smith to bring her up with him. When he arrived, I handed him an 'access all areas' pass. He looked at me and said, 'You're joking pal! I went and paid £80 for a ticket.'

Wayne grew up on the estate with us and would

never have been able to afford something like that or even have the chance to come behind the scenes. So for me to be able to thank him and give him that opportunity at the same time was a sincere pleasure.

He had never seen inside the changing rooms before and loved walking in with me and listening as Steve gave me my instructions.

'We want to give the first five rounds away, but make him work,' he reinforced. 'Extend him, Paul. Make him work more than he ever has before. He's only fought the full 12 round distance twice, so let's drag him into fucking deep waters.

'Naz is a fit fighter but his stamina is nothing compared to yours. We don't want him to do as he wants, we want to force him to do things he doesn't want to do. Understand?'

Whilst I nodded, I could see that Wayne looked very nervous and was sweating. In comparison, my nerves had disappeared in the days building up. I felt pretty relaxed and confident by that point and was just ready to get in the ring.

With about 15 minutes to go before the entrance, I did a few stretches and started taking some deep breaths to stretch my lungs. In the build up to the fight, everybody was talking about Naz's walk to the ring. Frank Maloney gave their camp a warning a few days before that if they took longer than five minutes, he would take me out and not bring me back until the posturing was over – it was no idle threat.

We got there and waited. Frank said, 'We'll leave this ring bang on five minutes if he's not here. They're trying to test us and if we just wait it shows weakness on our side.' Five minutes came and went, he gave it another 30 seconds and Naz was still not in the ring.

Maloney turned to me and said, 'Let's go.' And we

went back! Everybody stood there in absolute silence because of what we'd done.

Naz finally pulled up in a big 1960s American car and took a further five minutes to get to the ring. We made our point and it showed our strength of character.

Although my main focus was Naz, I couldn't help but take in the moment. Michael Buffer announcing, 'Let's get ready to rumble' as only he can, Joe Cortez in his 113th match as a referee calling the instructions and finishing with his tag line, 'I'm firm but I'm fair,' and tens of thousands of people screaming their heads off.

The hairs on the back of my neck were on end but the second the first bell rang, all the glitz and glamour disappeared, I had a job to do.

Initially, we traded pretty evenly but then I got hit with a left hook to the body followed by a left hook to the head. The moment I took that last punch I was rattled, down but not finished. My main concern was not actually the punch, but how my right ankle had fallen underneath me at a nasty angle.

My foot was almost facing the opposite way to what it should have been. I got onto one knee straight away to show I was ok, but also to take advantage of staying down for eight seconds. I could feel my ankle throbbing like mad, but the adrenaline took over and I jumped straight back into it.

Naz thought I was finished and spent about the next 40 seconds unloading on me heavily. My head was completely clear and the second I had a chance, I threw two left hooks to the body and a straight right, all of which landed, having a sobering effect and making him back off.

It was not the best start to a world title fight. My second ever knockdown and what X-rays would reveal later as severely torn tendons in my right ankle.

When I stood up for the second round and walked out, I felt like I had left my ankle in the corner. As a fighter who considered himself to be fairly good on his feet, when something like that happens you lose part of your defence because you can't attack in full.

The pain was bad, but I was not going to call this off. I blocked the ankle out of my mind for the rest of the fight.

Round four, I made some progress by drawing blood with a jab to Naz's nose. Rumours afterwards were that I'd actually broken it. However, in round six, he caught me with a shot to the body which was like a hot knife that went straight through me.

It was excruciating. If it hadn't have been in front of such a big crowd and for the world title, I may well have stayed down. I wanted to get up at about the count of two, but genuinely couldn't stand. It took every little bit of will-power to make that count.

I have to admit, things had not gone to plan by this stage of the fight. As I walked back to the corner, I knew that my punch rate was well under what I'd predicted and I just couldn't land cleanly. In fact, most of the time I couldn't land at all.

When you miss with a punch which is loaded with power, speed and adrenalin, you lose more energy than you would do connecting with it and mentally it starts to break up your confidence, especially in a fight like this where so much was at stake.

I was also starting to get tense, which was not great as that always ensures you get knackered quicker. He was trigger happy, not missing and his fancy footwork was pissing me off. It took everything I had to stay focused.

At last, round seven was a turning point. Instead of allowing Naz to steamroller me, I went on the attack and I could tell it slowed him down a bit – to the point where he stopped talking and clowning around.

The second I sat on the stool, Steve Pollard said, 'You've won that round! When he pulls away, that's when you're in danger. You're coming underneath well, so make sure you close him up and ram it in. Don't be fucking gentle, be rough, this is a fucking man's game. Take his balance and step on him. He keeps trying to measure you up, so keep moving and don't give him that chance.'

Halfway through the ninth round, I threw a perfectly timed left hook to the head which wobbled Naz and had the crowd on their feet screaming. He came back instantly but, unlike in round one, he didn't have as much fuel in the tank and I noticed his mouth was wide open and he kept rubbing his nose which was bleeding pretty heavily. I kept my foot on the gas and by the time the bell rung, I got a massive round of applause and knew that I'd bagged another round.

When I got back to the corner this time Pollard told me, 'The first 30 seconds of the next round are going to be dangerous because he's going to come after you. Keep your guard tight, keep moving and keep that pressure on him.'

The tenth round I was in total control. I landed straight right after straight right and caught him with some lovely left hooks. At the very end of the round, Naz hit the canvas but it was ruled a slip. Slip or not, I could tell he had taken a lot of punishment and was knackered. In all fairness, so was I.

Unfortunately, soon into the 11th, Naz caught me with a perfectly timed left hook to the head that sent me to the canvas. Although I got up, Joe Cortez made the decision to stop the fight.

The shot Naz finished me off with was not that hook, but the shot to the body in the sixth. I never fully recovered from it. Although everyone was saying Naz was the hardest hitting featherweight out there I'd disagree, his best qualities were his timing and accuracy. All through that fight, wherever I was, he would hit me, even when I thought I was out of distance. I take my hat off to him. However, judging by his face, I think he knew he'd been in a fight.

Frank Maloney came running over with Steve Pollard and said, 'I'm never happy to see any of my fighters lose, but I'm happy you lost fighting for the world title and putting in a performance of a lifetime. Nothing to be ashamed of. You left everything in the ring.'

Referee Cortez then came over to me and said, 'Whoever went down first was the one who was going to get stopped. You fought a great fight.'

I went back to my corner and the second after the doctor had given me the all clear, the first person to come over and embrace me was Naz. He leant over to my ear and uttered one word, 'Respect.' When he was interviewed later, he said to the media, 'Paul showed his heart. He went down, he got up. He can be a world champion.'

The fight was aired globally on HBO and within hours, Frank Maloney's phone was off the hook with offers for me. I knew I would fight for a world title again soon and remained optimistic about the future.

My brother, though, didn't take my defeat too well. He decided to drown his sorrows and walked into Manchester city centre on his own. After a few pints, he missed his coach home, the last train and ended up sleeping on a bench. When he woke up he also realised he'd spent all his money and ended up riding the train home without a ticket.

****

I QUICKLY came to terms with the defeat to Naz, it was not the end of the world for me. Although the days after I was limping, had two black eyes and it hurt every time I coughed, I was in a good state of mind. Obviously, I wasn't in the mood to go out partying although Scarborough Council had different plans.

Before the fight, the council gave me a pamphlet which outlined a parade around town that would happen, win, lose or draw. A big part of me knew that it was simply not right. Everyone was treating me like I'd beaten Naz, but I'd lost.

I decided to get over any remaining negativity by helping to put on a show for Scarborough, just to show my appreciation. A nice shiny Bentley had been organised to pick me up at my house, but I told them to meet me at my mum's house at Lismore Road, on the Edgehill estate.

I wanted my friends and family to benefit from the occasion as they'd always been behind me. I'll never forget their constant support, especially when I came back after my victory over Colin McMillan. They made massive banners on the fence railings saying 'Well done Paul. Edgehill – Home of the British Champion.' This was a small opportunity for me to repay that support.

I arrived about an hour before the car pulled up and there were already about 400 people waiting to see us off, with all the residents standing on their doorsteps waving and clapping. It was a great chance for me to chat with my mates, sign some memorabilia and have some photos taken with the people I grew up with. It was as special as the parade itself in my eyes.

We drove around town, before finishing off at the Town Hall for a reception. My mum was really shy and not used to being in front of so many journalists and cameras, but I think she loved the Bentley and waving to the thousands of fans from the comfort of the car.

It was great for me to be able to have her share in the experience because without her guidance and upbringing, none of it would have been possible. She was getting to experience the high life, which was priceless to me.

When we arrived, at the Town Hall, the guests were waiting and we received a massive round of applause. I said a big thank you to everyone for making me feel like a champion and promised I'd bring the world title home the next chance I fought for it.

The Mayor said, 'You have been a great ambassador for the town of Scarborough and we thank you from our hearts for that. We hope we can welcome you soon as world champion.'

Whilst everyone was enjoying the reception, my duties were not quite over, as I jumped back in the car and was driven straight to Scarborough Football Club's stadium to walk around the pitch at halftime.

Everyone kept shouting for me to raise my hand up like I'd won, but that didn't seem right. I wasn't comfortable with it. I got beat.

About a week after the parade, with the help of HBO's marketing and Frank Maloney's matchmaking, the likes of Kevin Kelley, Junior Jones and Manuel Medina were being mentioned by the boxing media as potential opponents for my next fight. I knew my second chance was not far away.

Around this time, I decided to visit a Mercedes Benz dealership as I wanted to test drive one of their sports cars. I walked in with my mates Wayne and Daz and saw a beautiful two-door convertible that would be perfect for a world champion.

All three of us were dressed in tracksuit bottoms, we each boasted shaven heads and were left standing at reception for about 15 minutes whilst everyone else was getting seen to. Daz was all for leaving but not me. We called over one of the salesmen and asked how much the convertibles were. He looked down his nose at us and gave us a hurried response which was of no help at all.

In the end, I said, 'I want to test drive one.'

Realising I wasn't leaving until that was sorted, he said, 'We don't have one available to test drive, but we might be able to get one in the next few weeks. If you give me your name and number, I'll call you when we have one on site.'

He dismissively asked, 'Surname?'

I replied, 'Ingle.'

He then said, 'First name?' and I told him, 'Paul.' He then said jokingly, 'Same name as the boxer who fought Prince Naseem last week, eh.'

I responded, 'That's right. But I'm healed up now.'

The penny suddenly dropped, he started grovelling and it became quite uncomfortable.

I was in a decent place yet life has a way of taking you off course when you least expect it, reminding you of your priorities in life. What happened next was like having a bucket of iced water chucked over me.

> **'I** actually thought before the Medina fight, 'He's got it all to do here.' Straight after the fight I said to myself, 'Wow – you got that wrong Nelson!"
>
> *- Johnny Nelson,*
> *Sky Sports Presenter & former*
> *cruiserweight world champion*

Round 11

☐

And the New...

AS kids, me and my brother were like chalk and cheese. He was well behaved and I was always the one getting into trouble, skiving school and giving my mum grief.

With me being three years older, I never used to let Dean hang out with me and my mates, although he'd always tag behind in the distance, but as we started to grow up together, we became very close.

We used to go out with our lurchers ferreting and rabbiting together but Dean used to give the fishing a miss as he simply wasn't patient enough.

When I was about 12, Dean decided to take up boxing. He used to come and watch me and one day put the gloves on and started to try and copy what I was doing. We sparred a few times and he would be chasing me round the ring trying to take my head off.

By that stage I had been boxing for nearly five years, was fairly ring crafty and was able to slip and duck most of his punches, however, you couldn't take your eyes off him for a second because he was relentless.

The Yorkshire Hunter

He used to get frustrated because he wanted to get stuck into me and I wasn't staying put long enough for him to do so. One time he said, 'What do you keep moving about for? Just stand there and stop moving your head so much!' We both laughed, but I still kept moving.

Some of the lads used to wind him up saying things like, 'You think you're tough because your brother is a champion.' He'd throw the gloves to the floor and challenge them to step outside and then take care of business.

Unfortunately some of the older kids, the mid-teenagers, used to take liberties with him when sparring because he was my brother and go really hard on him. I'd usually ask to spar with them straight after and, funnily enough, they never did again. I've always detested bullies.

When he was about 11, Dean did manage to focus himself and made us all very proud, winning the Yorkshire and Humberside divisional championships as an amateur. I won the same title alongside him for my age and weight category, making it a double Ingle success. Uncle Tubby and later on our two cousins, Jamie and George would also go on to win the same prize. Quite an achievement from one family and especially from one tiny boxing club.

Although Dean was a very good fighter, he didn't like the training and the regime that comes with boxing. Once, when he was competing, mum made him poached egg on toast a couple of hours before his fight because it was light, healthy and would digest quickly. Still hungry, he shot out to Irene's shop across the road and bought two packs of Black Jacks, those small chewy liquorice sweets which were a penny a go.

Later, when Dean was in the ring, after the first round of being beaten up, Tommy Johnson asked him if he was alright. Dean replied, 'Yeah,' then he chucked his guts up and out came all the Black Jacks. Tommy looked extremely worried thinking it was blood but soon got a whiff of the liquorice.

Unfortunately, as he entered his teenage years, the Edgehill estate provided him with more than enough temptation and opportunity for trouble. He started getting involved with local gangs and, within no time, was arrested by the police, almost always on Sundays. After a while I suggested he should to go to church instead.

When he was 13, Dean and his mates snuck past security to see the local bike races but one of the security guys spotted him, so he made a run for it. Whilst trying to sprint away, he fell down some stairs and almost down a 70-foot cliff.

What saved his life was his leg catching a massive fence spike which tore open his thigh and stopped him from rolling down any further. He broke his nose on the tumble down and his leg needed over 30 stitches and a few weeks in hospital before he could properly walk again.

On another occasion, aged 16, he was on a motorbike with a mate of his on the back and was flying down a road on the estate, when he hit a moving car head on. The lad behind Dean went flying over him but, because he was wearing a crash helmet, somehow managed to hit the ground head first, bounce off the concrete and walk away without a scratch. Dean wasn't wearing any protective gear and went flying into a hedge.

It took an hour for the ambulance to come, during which time Dean was in and out of consciousness and was a real bloody mess. When we got to the hospital, we all thought he'd lost his teeth, but when they showed us the X-ray, it became clear that his top row had been hit so hard, they had been smashed right up into his gums. He needed major surgery to get everything fixed but, in all honesty, he was lucky to be alive.

Dean continued to mix with the wrong crowds and was getting sucked deeper and deeper into a side of life we didn't want to see him in. His reputation became so bad that whenever something happened in the local area, the police would often come knocking on our front door as their first port of call.

He got accused of attempted murder once because he had a gun in the house. The police tied him up and pushed him face down into the grass in the garden in front of me and my mum. It was horrible to witness. They soon realised they had the wrong person and let him go shortly after. They tried the same with a robbery at the post office mum was working at and again let him go after realising he was not involved.

The defining moment which turned his life around very nearly almost finished it. A couple of weeks after the Naz fight, he was in a nightclub and he spotted a lad who was trying to sell drugs to a couple of youngsters. Dean told him to pack it in and they ended up getting in a bit of a scuffle. After they'd finished scrapping, he thought that was the end of it and walked away.

When he came out, he was surprised to see this lad waiting for him in an alleyway and calling him over. They started fighting again and Dean ended up getting stuck into him on the floor. The other guy started to hit back and Dean thought he was being caught with light punches to his back, but he was actually being stabbed with a broken bottle. As Dean got off him, thinking the other guy had had enough, the lad sprinted away.

Dean was wearing a cream shirt that night and as he came out of the alleyway, hundreds of people were all leaving the nightclub and several started screaming. Dean wondered why and suddenly realised he was the centre of attention. He then looked down to see blood pumping out the bottom of his boots.

People were calling for an ambulance, but thankfully there was a lady taxi driver who knew Dean and she could tell how serious it was and didn't wait for it to arrive. Instead, she put him straight in her cab and bolted off to A&E, saving his life.

One of my mates who had been at the club called me straight away and I drove down to the hospital and met them as fast as I could. By the time I'd got to the hospital, Dean was high on pain killers and in a deep sleep. He was then taken to theatre straight away to be worked on by the surgeons as the stabbings had just missed an artery and he ended up staying in hospital for a couple of weeks.

At a time when I thought that nothing could take the shine off the quality of my life, that incident brought everything down to earth with a bang. Health and family are the most important things. When both come into a crisis at the same time, you start to realise that all the money and status in the world means nothing.

The stabbing acted as a wake-up call for Dean and from that point, he really got himself together. I remember him saying, 'I'm really sorry Paul. Every time I get in trouble, your name is the first thing to be associated with the incident. I'm tired of giving grief to mam and I'm going to get myself together.'

It takes a hell of a lot of character to turn things around the way he did and I'm very proud of him. He met a great woman and started a family and he never missed one of my fights as either an amateur or a pro. It meant the world to me to have him ringside when I fought, although boxing was easy compared to what he'd been through.

The Yorkshire Hunter

About a week after Dean was released from hospital, I had a near-death experience – or so I thought. Scarborough is known for being Britain's first ever seaside resort and although we do have the occasional day of rain, wind and cloud, when the sun comes out, the beaches are packed and the atmosphere is something else. I'd decided, with my earnings from the Naz fight, to buy myself a little toy. It was a high-powered jet ski that did about 60 mph and I was ready to be the next David Hasselhoff and audition for *Baywatch*.

On this particular Saturday, Dean and my mates came down to the beach and we all had a blast with my new toy although I'm not sure Dean should have been out there, with his wound all strapped up and goodness knows how many stitches which were apparently supposed to have been kept dry.

Rocky Rowe then turned up and decided to have a go, which provided entertainment for everyone. He's a big lad and we didn't have a vest to fit him.

Wearing a pair of jeans and a shirt, he rolled his trousers up and then took off at full speed in a straight line, heading for Holland. It turned out there was a fault with the steering, which only allowed him to slightly turn the jet ski. He did a massive u-turn about half a mile wide to come back and we were all laughing like mad by the time he finally pulled up.

After sorting the steering, I turned to the lads and said, 'Watch and learn boys. This is how you ride a jet ski.' The sea was flat like a mirror and the sun shining, which meant you could see for miles. I took off at full speed, spinning it left and right and showing off with any other stunts I could pull off.

The next thing, as I'm doing about 30 miles an hour, about 20 shark fins started appearing around me. As I turned to the left, they turned to the left. As I turned right, they did the same thing. I turned the jet ski round and drove back fast and headed straight to the shore.

When I hit the sand the jet ski continued to go on for about 50 feet and the people sunbathing were diving off their deckchairs thinking I was going to hit them.

I then jumped off and started shouting and pointing out at sea, 'Shaaaaarks! Shaaaaaaaarks!'

Somebody calmly said, 'They're porpoises.'

I breathlessly replied, 'Are they a deadly type of shark then?'

'No – they're like dolphins.'

Everybody laughed hysterically. Nowadays they have become fairly common in Scarborough, but in those days, they weren't very well known – that was my excuse anyway.

****

SOON after the Naz fight, I had been scheduled to take on Alex Moon but the tendons in my ankle needed at least eight weeks off from intense training, so we had to cancel.

Frank Maloney then hit me with some fantastic news. He asked me if I'd like another shot at Naz, swiftly followed by, 'What about if I get you a crack at Manuel Medina's IBF world title and get Sky to cover it? If you beat him, not only will you become world champion, but Naz will definitely want that rematch to unify the division.'

Medina was certainly not a walk in the park. In fact, going into the fight, I was a heavy underdog. He had been world champion for a number of sanctioning bodies since 1991, had contested 14 world title bouts, losing only three and had taken some serious scalps along the way.

He was a class fighter and a very tough Mexican. The

fact that he was threatening to knock me out in under four rounds was also quite worrying.

I was desperate to have the fight in Scarborough. To be able to win the world title for the community I loved and respected so much and the chance to really put the town on the sporting map meant everything to me.

Unfortunately the local council didn't feel the same. The fight cost around £20,000 to stage and I was gobsmacked when they said they only were willing to put a grand towards it. At first I thought it was a joke but it never happened.

Frank Maloney and I even offered to put £5,000 each of our own cash towards covering half the outlay but Scarborough Council still wasn't interested. I have to say, I felt let down.

In the end, the venue and date were sorted. I would be challenging Manuel Medina for the IBF world title at the Ice Arena in Hull on the 13 November, 1999. Having trained there since turning pro five years before and always been treated incredibly well by everyone in the city, it was a great alternative and I didn't feel too bad that my fans only had to travel about 50 miles.

Medina was not coming over to England just to pick up his pay cheque, he was looking to do exactly the same. We'd both lost to Naz in the same round and wanted a rematch to set the record straight. Most fighters would come a week before when fighting overseas, he arrived three weeks early.

Headlines of, 'It's Make or Break for Ingle' started appearing about eight weeks before the Medina fight. I'd earned a lot of respect against Naz but if I lost against Medina, everybody, the press especially, would start to brand me as a nearly man who challenged for world titles, but never really got there – somebody who was a good boxer but could never really mix it with the big boys. The pressure of potentially losing two world title challenges back-to-back was immense.

I was in the best physical shape I'd ever been and it didn't happen by accident. About six weeks before the Medina fight, I hired Neil Featherby as my conditioner.

He came with a great pedigree, having worked with people such as footballer Danny Mills, a number of top rugby players and a long list of boxers, including Herbie Hide. Neil was on the road with me for every step. Having run a crazy number of marathons in very fast times and ultra-marathons, this was certainly someone who was fit enough to push me, yet not wreck my body during the process.

Neil was also a sports psychologist, so apart from making me stronger and fitter, he gave me a new level of self-belief and confidence and got me thinking like a world champion before I'd even won the crown.

We would discuss how my previous workouts had gone but he would never butter me up. If I wasn't doing something right, he would tell me straight and that's what I really appreciated.

I was about two stone over my fighting weight a couple of months before the Medina fight, which was normal, and with Neil on board, he was able to make sure I lost the excess sensibly. Although I was dropping weight, I was not losing any strength or essential fluids. As fight night approached I was in incredible condition.

In between, I took every opportunity to put something back into the local community. Being able to raise money for great causes such as National Children's Homes and Age Concern, among others, was the least I could do for the community which had gone out on a limb for me.

Although I wasn't going to be fighting in

The Yorkshire Hunter

Scarborough, I made sure that all my training was on home turf. We set up camp with an 18-foot ring in the Empress Suite at the Grand Hotel, which had an incredible view overlooking the ocean. Although sparring was open to the public, it was a no frills set up, exactly how I wanted it.

Rough and ready wasn't everyone's taste. I had a nice pool of sparring partners, including Terry Morrill, Danny Hunt, Kevin Lear, Chris Hooper, Gary Steadman and Graham Earl. Although Terry was a middleweight and Graham a lightweight, none of them ever took liberties or once complained about the conditions. My main sparring partner, Scott Harrison, couldn't stand the set up though.

First day in sparring, he was trying to take my head off and, as much as I wanted to get stuck in, I was also aware I didn't want to pick up any unnecessary injuries. After a couple of rounds I started to respond in kind. Second day, Harrison stormed off and said he didn't like the place and the open sparring.

On fight night you are in front of thousands of people, so what's the difference? If the public started to act up, Steve Pollard would have put a stop to it in a heartbeat. I was happy to see the back of Harrison. I needed positive people around me and he certainly wasn't one.

Steve Pollard's patience, not something he was renowned for anyway, was also not the greatest around this time. Jimmy Savile came into the suite right in the middle of a sparring session, smoking a massive cigar. Then a local celebrity, Steve let him know exactly what he thought and he can be pretty intimidating. Savile walked out pretty quickly.

We replaced Harrison with Toncho Tonchev, who was an Olympic silver medallist and would go on to win a stack of titles himself, including European and WBU world crowns. Toncho was no fuss – just a nice down to earth lad.

Although he was not the biggest puncher, he was technically incredible with his distance and timing, stood the same height as Medina – four inches taller than me – and really made me work to get under his jab to reduce his range. In the meantime, Medina had brought over his own sparring partners from Mexico to put him through his paces, including future world champion, light welterweight, Humberto Soto.

****

THE press conference, also held at the Grand Hotel, was probably one of the most pleasant I'd ever taken part in or witnessed.

Medina was a lovely guy and I got on with him before and after the fight. He never once tried to take a cheap shot in the media and was very complimentary of both my amateur and pro boxing careers.

He had vowed to beat me for Mexico. It was nothing personal, simply to do with the fact that Naz had beaten César Soto in a scrappy fight a few weeks before and he wanted to do his country, a fanatical boxing nation, proud.

On the way up to the conference, I decided to stop at the local chippie. When I walked in, I handed over freshly wrapped fish and chips, with lashings of salt and vinegar and said, 'A present for you.' He had never seen anything like it before, but tucked in, gave me the thumbs up and said, 'Good.'

When the time came to do the photo-opportunity face off, Rocky Rowe's 11 year-old-son was standing in between us, dressed in a poncho with a fake moustache and a big sombrero pretending to split us up.

Although we'd been well behaved and in good spirits, the moment I got close and looked into Medina's eyes it suddenly became apparent who exactly was in front of me. Although he was only supposed to be two years older than me, rumours were that he was at least five more and possibly eight. He had a very hard looking face with swelling and scaring built up over a near 70-fight pro career. I knew at that exact moment that this was not going to be easy.

We shook hands once again and then I decided to watch the England versus Scotland football match in the bar with the fans. I felt very calm and relaxed and it was nice to be able to cheer on England – and they won which seemed like a good omen.

The night before, I was genuinely shocked with the number of good luck messages sent directly to both mine and my mum's house. It was unbelievable. Lennox Lewis had even taken the time before his rematch against Holyfield to wish me the best.

Talking to the *Daily Star* he'd said, 'Tell him from me that the next time we meet I hope we'll both be world champions. And I know he can do it. He has the guts and the determination. And he has already shown that he has the talent.' It was another nice boost so close to the fight.

On the night, as expected, the atmosphere was incredible. It was a much smaller crowd than the Naz one, but they sounded even louder.

Just before leaving the changing room, Steve Pollard briefed me on tactics once again.

'This is yours for the taking,' he impressed on me. 'He won't be unpredictable like Naz, but he will be all over you from the start. Take ownership of the ring like you did against Colin, get under his jab and work that body.'

Little did I know, but Pollard had bet his entire wage packet on me to win.

I was introduced by Michael Buffer, as 'the pride of

Yorkshire' and, from the off, we went to work. From the first bell, Medina wanted to dictate his range and workrate. I realised I needed to break his rhythm on both fronts, keep in his face and make him uncomfortable.

I landed a massive left hook that almost lifted him off the ground and soon after a beautiful counter.

Medina wanted to tap gloves at the end of the round, but instead, I gave him a stare. Despite the fact that we had been friendly in the build-up, in between those four ropes he was my enemy and the person holding my belt. I needed to get any psychological advantage I could.

Second round, I caught him with a right hook to the jaw, followed by a left hook and he went down. Medina banged the canvas, angry with himself, but his eyes were still a hundred per cent clear.

All those years ago when I was a kid in the amateurs, I used to bang about a thousand left hooks into the medicine ball with Ray Simpson. Nothing else – just the left hook. At the time I couldn't always understand why we'd do it, especially when my arm felt like a lump of lead the next morning. That night I realised why.

I still needed to be cautious though, although the crowd was shouting for me to go for the knockout, I knew that was a trap Medina was waiting for me to fall into. That said, about a minute later I caught him with another left hook to the chin and knocked him down again. At that point, it was becoming more tempting to look for a quick finish because the three knockdown rule was in effect. Nonetheless, I kept my wits about me. Two rounds in and I was four points up.

Rounds three to five, in terms of pace, were unbelievable. Medina showed why he was a long-time champion as he started to get his rhythm going again. Although I could see openings to hit, he kept making it more and more awkward for me to land. He was reading me and in a second changing his game plan.

Unfortunately, disaster struck. You can be the best fighter in the world but if you suffer a cut it can flip a fight in a matter of seconds. The last minute of the fifth round turned out to be very messy and when I got back to the corner, Mick Williamson, my cut man, really had to get to work.

I had a large swelling under my left eye, a cut just under the left eyebrow and a nasty one on my scalp due to a clash of heads. Although I wasn't hurt, the blood was streaming down into my eyes, I'd been careless, it was unforgiveable.

In the eighth, Medina held on for a moment and, whilst in close, I looked at his face, his eyes were badly swollen and his lips were cut up. I thought he had to slow down but he didn't. Instead, he kept bouncing around throwing punches. If I'd taken my foot of the gas for a single second he would have been all over me.

About 30 seconds into round 10, I threw a right hand straight through the middle of Medina's guard which caught him flush on the chin and knocked him down into the ropes. Out of all the moments in the fight, this was the closest he was to being badly hurt.

He was really struggling to get steady on his feet and I started to unload as heavily as I could. His left eye was almost closed but he just kept fighting back. Never in my life had I seen something like this, it was something else – he just seemed to create new energy all the time like a robot.

Although the cut over my left my eye was affecting my vision throughout the 12th, I felt confident that I had everything in hand. I was knackered in all fairness, but I managed to dance around, staying out of harm's way, just to take me to the finishing line.

With about 30 seconds to go, he caught me with a right hand bang on the cut over my left eye. It wasn't even that hard a punch, I was just incredibly tired.

I took the full eight count and then rose to my feet. The last 20 seconds were the longest of my life. I just kept thinking, 'Everything I've done in the last 11-and-a-half rounds could disappear here.'

Thankfully, I managed to clear my head and get out of the way of Medina's power shots until the bell sounded by which time, the crowd had erupted on the assumption that I'd won.

The second it was over, Medina came and gave me a big hug and told me he'd never been hooked to the body so hard before. He also picked up my hand and walked me around the ring. The sign of a true champion and a gentleman.

I later found out that we'd made it into the record books for the number of punches in one fight. We jointly threw over 2,000 and also made it into the 400 club for the number that landed.

The stadium went from deafening cheers to absolute silence as the judges' scorecards were being read out, then back to deafening cheers as the ring announcer said those words every boxer wants to hear, 'All three in favour of, and the neeeeeww......' After the word 'new', the arena exploded in sound and colour.

From the moment the Medina fight had been announced, I'd started to have dreams of this moment over and over again.

So much so, I woke up almost in tears wanting it so badly. I thought about Medina so often he may as well have been living in my house because my dreams were that vivid.

Now it was real. Hearing the words, 'new....world

champion…Scarborough….' and having the ref lifting my hand – it was a million times better than the dream.

Who would have ever thought that a kid from the Edgehill estate, who stepped into the gym as a chubby lad all those years ago, would end up holding a world title? It was unreal. Now I could say I was the champion. Now I could celebrate.

Later that night, I went back to Steve Pollard's boozer in Hull. Half of Scarborough travelled with us. Contrary to what many may think, I hardly had anything to drink that night, not least because I'd just been through bloody hell. Also, I wanted to stay up to watch the Lewis-Holyfield re-match and I had duties the day after.

****

AS kids, we used to always know who was going to be turning on the Christmas lights in Scarborough as it'd be in all the papers. Never did I think it would be me. When I woke up in the morning in Hull, I was driven back to my mum's where I did an interview with the *Scarborough Evening News*, before heading off to the Brunswick Shopping Centre in town, to turn on the lights with Bruce Jones, Les Battersby from *Corrie*. It was a surname that I would hear a lot more.

In all honesty, it was a bit of a gamble accepting to turn on the lights before the result of the Medina fight was known.

Despite putting on an act for everybody, I looked and felt like crap. Most of my smashed-up face was covered up with a pair of massive sunglasses and I could barely move. My muscles had seized up, the cuts and bruises were now very sore and everything I did was in small moves and in plenty of pain.

My team had suggested a massage but I was so tender, there was no way that was ever going to happen. Everyone wanting to shake my blown-up hands certainly didn't help either.

However, the second I walked into the Brunswick, the cheers and amount of people who turned out to congratulate me certainly took my mind off the pain. I've never liked taking tablets of any sort and hate needles, so I went without painkillers and just stuck with it as long as I could. After barely a couple of hours I went back home and straight to bed.

When I got to the bedroom, I put the IBF belt under the bed for safekeeping and then passed out for about 12 hours. The first thing I did when I woke up was to check it was still there and if what I'd achieved was real. It was a nice moment.

I watched the Medina fight again in the comfort of my lounge on the sofa, whilst putting my hands into bowls of hot and then ice water to reduce the swelling. It was nice to hear some of the compliments from Sky's Glenn McCrory and Spencer Oliver. Little did I know I would have more than boxing in common with Spencer in little over a year's time.

Exactly a week after the Medina fight, Scarborough Borough Council had another parade lined up for me. By now I'd managed to get rid of most of the aches and pains with some light exercise and stretching and my face looked near normal again.

I even did an interview with the *Daily Star* and sent out a message to Naz saying, 'Get back in training – give me a few weeks off and we'll get it back on.'

As with the last parade, we set off from Edgehill but this time all my team were with me, including Neil Featherby, Frank Maloney and Steve Pollard. Frank had kindly organised for a chauffeur-driven Rolls Royce for me and my mum and we also had a group of police on motorbikes to escort us into town, where an open-top bus was waiting for us.

Everyone had piled into the town centre. We turned a corner and there was a sea of thousands of people screaming and shouting the second they saw us. Shops had banners with some lovely messages hanging from their windows and the sounds of clicking cameras was unbelievable.

This was the first time a boxer from Scarborough had won a world title. Most people who experience fame tend to leave their roots but not me. I was very proud. Although the parade was a celebration of me winning the title, I felt it was for the town.

Holding the world title belt above my head was incredible. To this day, if I close my eyes I can still hear the cheers from the crowds.

After about an hour we stepped off the bus for a reception at the Town Hall. It took about 20 minutes before it could start as I was mobbed by fans for autographs and photos.

The reception looked like it had been catered for with a £20 budget. When they said, 'Raise your glass', they literally meant glass. In terms of food, there was a bag of crisps in a bowl and some nuts. Thankfully, the social club down the Seamer Road had organised a proper celebration later that evening and I was able to let my hair down.

The day after, I'd noticed a missed call from my mate Mark Legge and decided to give him a call back. After ringing a few times, it went through to his voicemail which was, 'and the neeeeew, featherweight champion of the world, Paaaaaaaaul Innnnnnnngle!'

It had been recorded from the television after the Medina fight and was so long it cost about ten quid before you could actually leave a reply. It certainly made me laugh.

As 1999 drew to a close, I was on the verge of releasing some great news about my next fight. I could have probably done with a few months more to recharge myself, but this opportunity was the stuff dreams are made of.

> '**P**aul Ingle - he's one of
> the toughest sons of
> bitches I ever fought.'
> — *Junior Jones,*
> *former featherweight*
> *world champion*

Round 12

□

Madison Square Garden

ALTHOUGH winning the IBF world title against Medina was possibly the best moment of my life, financially, it didn't produce the goods in terms of ticket sales. My fans were incredible and made up the bulk of the 1,600 who attended but unfortunately the 3,000 sell out which we all expected just didn't happen and Panix Promotions took a big hit.

It was now a catch-22 situation, big fights meant travelling but I also didn't want to stray too far from Scarborough or Yorkshire. In the meantime, Frank Maloney had sent a copy of the Medina fight to HBO to gauge their interest.

It was looking likely that Naz would fight Junior Jones and I would take on South Africa's Viyani Bungu. As it turned out, Naz fought Bungu and I took on Jones! I ended up commentating on Naz's fight against Bungu for Sky Sports and was rooting for him to win, not just because he was a Yorkshireman, but because I was dying for the rematch.

When Frank broke the news to me of my next fight being against Junior Jones he mentioned that I would have to go out to the USA. Junior was holding the IBO world title at the time, so the opportunity to hold two belts and get one step closer to unifying the division was a real draw.

Frank paused before then dropping the real news. 'You'll be fighting at Madison Square Garden on the same bill as Lennox Lewis and Arturo Gatti.'

My heart dropped through my guts. Every boxer dreams of fighting in Vegas or the Garden for a world title.

From Maloney's perspective, this was also an historic moment as he became the first English manager to ever have three English fighters – all of whom he'd signed from the amateurs – fighting three Americans on the same bill at Madison Square Garden; Scott Harrison, Lewis and yours truly.

First chance I had, I let my close friends and family know. I genuinely wasn't expecting anyone to come over and had to be careful the way I came across so that it didn't look like I was boasting or they were missing out on something special.

Most of them had debts and very few owned their own cars or houses. In fact I told most of them to just tune in and watch me on the television, because I felt guilty of the amount of money it would cost them.

Daz Smith summed them up, though. As I started to say to him, 'Don't worry if you can't come out......,' he interrupted, put his hand on my shoulder and said, 'We grew up together in the 1970s as little kids watching the likes of Sugar Ray Leonard and Muhammad Ali fight at Madison Square Garden. To see our mate from the Edgehill estate fighting out there, at the Mecca of boxing, defending his world title is something I wouldn't miss for the world.

'I can't afford to go Paul. None of us can. For many of the people coming to support you, they don't even have passports and this will probably be their first and only time they will fly. But we'll work extra shifts and borrow if need be to cheer you on. We're not missing this for the world and nothing you say can change that.'

I was choked.

****

THE training camp for this fight was superb and to make it even better, it was again all based in Scarborough. Before Neil Featherby came on board, I would often lose my high level of fitness very quickly between fights and also put on a lot of weight, but not this time round.

Neil also worked on my psychology for this fight. If the weather was really bad or I was demotivated for whatever reason, Neil would say, 'When you are in the later rounds and you are looking at your opponent and can't quite figure him out, wondering if he is knackered – deep down inside you are getting knackered.

'Going for a run in the rain will seem like a nice place to be in comparison. When you feel like stopping, just think that Jones is running the streets of New York in the freezing cold. Do the training now so you have no doubt in the ring.'

Junior Jones was already a legend, having been the first person to hand out back-to-back losses against one of my heroes, Marco Antonio Barrera, at a time when Barrera was already a very well-established champ in his prime.

The way Jones could combine his speed, power and variation of punches was magical. We, therefore, tried to take some of that away. We decided to focus on making him feel uncomfortable by getting underneath his jab and working angles. We also realised that Jones would not be an open target, so we practised throwing shots to the arms, heart and shoulders in advance of throwing the big left hooks or overhand rights.

The time had come to fly over to the USA. We went out a week before and thankfully this time there was no drama with exploding engines on the planes or emergency landings on airbases. Although the way Kenny Brock was behaving you would have thought so. He was terrified of flying and the moment he sat down on the plane, opened the passenger pack that the stewardess gave him and wore every piece of gear they'd provided.

Earmuffs, DVT socks, ear plugs, eye mask, you name it. If they had a parachute, he would have strapped that to his back also. Steve Pollard on the other hand used his tried-and-tested method of complimentary booze to get him through the flight.

Once landed in New York, we drove straight to the hotel in Manhattan. I remember paying for a really nice suite for me and my girlfriend at the time. The keys were handed to me, we got to our room and I was a little disappointed as it wasn't as flash as I'd hoped.

Next thing, the phone went and it was my brother Dean. 'Paul, these rooms are unbelievable!' he was shouting. 'The room is like a mini-hotel. Top floor, jacuzzi, four sofas, incredible view. This is the life.'

Before he could even finish, there was a knock on his door and me standing outside – they'd given it to the wrong Ingle.

Unfortunately, it didn't last very long for me either as I was bombarded with prank calls in the middle of the night and ended up moving rooms on three occasions.

One late afternoon, the phone started to ring off the hook and I was just about at breaking point. I was just about to have a right go at whoever it was when I heard the voice

Above: What a backdrop! Pictured against my beloved Scarborough.

Left: John Prescott MP splits Manuel Medina and me up prior to our scrap in November 1999.

Below: Facing the press afterwards.

Below left: After becoming double world champ at Madison Square Garden - with Glenn McCrory, April 2000.

Above: I've done it! Newly-crowned IBF champion in November 1999.

Rght: Pictured with Steve Pollard straight after the Medina fight.

Below: Open-top bus celebrations with the Lord Mayor in Scarborough. It doesn't get better than that.

ON THE ATTACK ... Paul Ingle lands a right to the chin of rival Jonjo Irwin

COUNTER-ATTACK ... Jonjo Irwin (left) puts the pressure on Paul Ingle

THE LISTENER ... Ingle in his corner

ON THE ATTACK ... Ingle wears down Moussa Sangare at Hull

INGLE IS WORLD CLASS!

Mike Tyas reports

PAUL Ingle's destruction of Moussa Sangare went exactly to plan last night.

It was a world class performance, Paul is so that league new, and trainer Steve Pollard after Ingle had won his rival after 10 rounds of their IBF world inter-continental featherweight title fight in the Hull Arena.

Ingle's boss Frank Maloney was also full of praise for the classy Scarborough boxer. "It was first-class," he said.

"It was the best since he fought and won the British title against Colin McMillan."

"Sangare was a world class opponent and a good name for Paul to hang on his record."

Ingle agreed the fight went according to the script. "I threw body shots, combinations and jabs to break him up," he said.

"I knew in the end he could not take the shots I was hitting him with."

Ingle is still pushing for a world featherweight title bout against IBO champion Radford Beasley, but says his options open by announcing he will favours a title tilt at Billy Hardy for the European crown.

"I would like to fight him. He's got the European title and I want it," he said.

Maloney was due to have talks today with directors of his promotional company, Panix Promotions.

But with the last two fights in Hull making big financial losses, Maloney might see a fight against Hardy possibly in London as a safer bet, rather than the opposite financial risk of bringing another show up north.

Wherever the next fight is staged however, Maloney has said it would not be in August — the date he originally announced months ago for a possible scrap at The Spa in Scarborough.

Maloney has a running contract with Sky Sports and 1 August is not free for them to stage a boxing show.

This page and overleaf: A collection of press cuttings from a never less than eventful boxing career.

NOW I'LL TAKE ON THE WORLD

REPORT: Neil Pickford and Mike Tyas

SCARBOROUGH boxer Paul Ingle needs YOUR help to realise his dream of fighting for a world title in his home town.

Last night Ingle beat Mousa Sangare to become the new IBF World Inter-Continental Featherweight champion and set up a potential world title fight against American Radford Beasley at the Spa.

But promoter Frank Maloney has threatened to stage the fight somewhere else unless Ingle's fans show their support and prove it will be worth his while to bring the Scarborough and Sheffield-based champion back to his roots.

HUNTING FOR HARDY ... Paul Ingle is ready for his European title battle with Billy Hardy

VICTORY ... Paul after last night's bout

● Leugton .... page two
● Comment .... page six
● Report and pictures .... centre pages
                        .... back page
● World Class.

Ingle hits top ten in WBC rankings

BRITISH featherweight champ Paul Ingle (left) can now officially fight for the world title after starring up the rankings.

The city-boxer has broken through into the top ten of the World Boxing Council's listings.

They have installed him as number six in the world which means he could eventually take on the unbeaten Prince Naseem Hamed.

This is a welcome boost before Ingle's next defence of his title on October 11 at Sheffield Arena.

If he beats Jon Jo Irwin he will win a Lonsdale belt outright.

But his bout is just one of a star-studded line-up which includes Hamed and Steve Collins.

He said: "It will be good to be part of a night which has so much exposure and it will be great to see Hamed up close and watch how he fights, but obviously I will be concentrating on my fight first of all.

"I will be focused on what I have got to do and then I will be looking forward to a European feather-

weight title fight against Billy Hardy, as long as he does not lose his fight on October 4."

Ingle, who is now fighting out of the Millennium Sports Centre, Dalton Street Industrial Estate, was delighted about his new ranking.

He has been sparring against European under-19 featherweight champion Scott Harrison.

The public are welcome to watch him spar between 3pm-4pm until Thursday, and tickets for his fight are available.

RIDING
HIGH ... Paul,
his mum Carol
and fiancée Sam Cockson
set off for the
Town Hall in a Bentley

You're our champion

Ingle hits back as Naz lays down challenge...

I'LL FIGHT YOU, IF PRICE IS RIGHT

FIGHT OPTIONS ...
Paul Ingle

Exclusive by Mike Tyas

DEFIANT Paul Ingle has told Naseem Hamed to put his money where his mouth is if the world champion wants to take him on.

European champ Ingle revealed to promoter Frank

BIG FIGHT SPECIAL

He came,
he saw, he
conquered

YOUR FULL TV, SATELLITE TV AND RADIO LISTINGS ARE ON PAGE 13 TODAY

BIG FIGHT SPECIAL

Paul's punch-power silences New York

Mike Tyas
SPORTS
NEW YORK

INGLE

Mike Tyas' scorecard

Editorial-Advertising ... 723 363838 Classified Ads 01723 363838

Evening News, Friday 12 November 1999 - 15

Evening News special on tomorrow's world showdown

INGLE
v
MANUEL MEDINA

IBF FEATHERWEIGHT CHAMPIONSHIP OF THE WORLD 13th NOVEMBER 1999

1 DAY TO GO

Forget Scotland v England – this is the big one

PRINCE RE-MATCH THE BIG PRIZE

Ringside
report and
pictures
... in
Monday's
Evening
News

NOT THIS TIME ... Manuel Medina is floored by a Naseem Hamed hook during their WBO world title showdown in Dublin in August 1996. The referee stepped in to stop the fight in the 11th round.

Scrapbook:
The press
followed
the twists
and turns
of my
career with
interest.

Ingle Spas with fans

GOOD LUCK PAUL

Evening News

High-profile adventures: I will always be grateful for the loyal support of my local newspapers.

Hero's welcome as Ingle returns with world title after bloody 12-round battle

CHAMPION

Our hero!

Joining the jet set

IT'S not only in the ring that boxing star Paul Ingle is making a splash these days.

The Scarborough featherweight, who takes on champion Manuel Medina for the IBF world crown in Hull on Saturday night, has taken time out from his tough training routine to get in some practice on his jet ski.

Photographer Kevin Allen has pictured Paul heading back for the beach after a high-speed session on the seas.

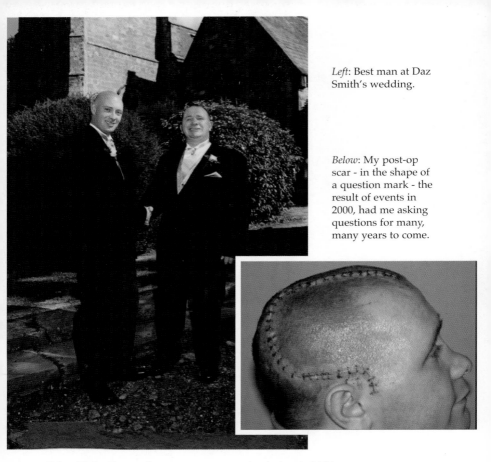

Left: Best man at Daz Smith's wedding.

Below: My post-op scar - in the shape of a question mark - the result of events in 2000, had me asking questions for many, many years to come.

Below: Ricky Hatton shows support at my fundraiser in 2007.

Above: Reception duties at the Paul Ingle Boxing Academy, Hull.

Below: WBC presents me with an award. Left to right, David Walker, Steve Collins, me and Sonny Pollard. February 2014.

Left: Receiving ABA creditation with Lee Stephenson and Sonny.

Right: Presenting the Masters belt to Danny Brown after working Sonny Pollard's corner, in December 2014.

Below: With nephew Harry, brother Dean, Sonny, Dan Gregory and Paul Zanon in November 2014.

of Dick Tingle. Although that could have been the name of a prankster, he was a good, honest writer from the *Hull Daily Mail* who had covered my career since my first amateur trophy.

With only a week to go before fight night, we spent the remaining days keeping fit with some runs through Central Park and pad work. I was actually surprised with how fresh the air was, I was convinced the pollution would be overwhelming.

One thing that did strike me about three days before the fight was the people walking around the streets. One afternoon, I was stretching my legs, just taking in the sights down Fifth Avenue with Neil, when I thought I was in Scarborough. The number of fans who had come over was unbelievable. From the other side of the street they started chanting my name, it was astonishing but at the same time pretty strange.

Whilst I was getting over jet lag by training and adjusting my sleeping patterns, the lads were mixing it with the locals and telling me tales of eating 20oz steaks and limitless buffets. Nice, but it had got to the point where I was having to improvise to satisfy my hunger.

On one occasion, I'm sure Neil thought I'd lost the plot. We were sitting in the hotel room chatting about the routine when I turned to him and said, 'Do you fancy a pint?' He looked at me strangely but I made out I was holding a pint of lager and started to drink it, gulping and swallowing loudly, all the way to the end of the imaginary glass. I then turned to Neil and said, 'I really needed that.' We both burst into fits of laughter.

With only two days to go, things hotted up – press interviews at the top of the Empire State Building, a visit to Madison Square Garden before the big night and the weigh-in.

The Yorkshire Hunter

The interviews went well, although they kept us waiting two hours and there was a 40-minute queue to get in. However, the visit to Madison Square Garden was something else.

I managed to do a bit of pad work with Steve Pollard in the ring and couldn't help looking around in between breaks, checking out the photos of past boxing greats who had fought there, dating from the early 1900s. To think I was going to step through the ropes and be added was almost mind-blowing.

Yet, the fight almost never happened.

I could accept silly things like prank calls, or the fact that I was an underdog in my opponent's back yard, or even that all three judges for the fight were from the Big Apple. But when the New York State Athletic Commission demanded the weigh-in to be 12 hours before the fight, I flipped.

With all the concerns around the world of boxers being dehydrated before fights, this was a crazy suggestion, but if we'd have known this was the case at the time of signing contracts then we would have prepared accordingly.

I'd been preparing for 15 weeks for a 24-hour weigh-in. To move it forward was a very big deal. They changed the plans just four days before the fight which was unforgiveable. To top it off, Jones had now booked into the same hotel.

When I went down to the lobby, I had people looking round corners for me, checking he wasn't there. I didn't want to look at him, never mind speak to him, until I was in the ring.

I was genuinely prepared to pull out if they enforced this lead-in time. Even the British Boxing Board of Control jumped in and backed me up. Unfortunately, the NYSAC overruled everybody, including the IBF and the IBO.

It was a very tense time and in the end it was Frank Maloney who laid it on the line to me.

'It's your first time in the US and yes they are playing around, but we have to go with it or call it off and you'll get stripped of your title. You are in great shape, so let's do the weigh-in and do the rest in the ring tomorrow. Make him pay in the ring. Rise above this, Paul. Show you are the better man and the better champion.'

Although it went against the grain, I agreed to their conditions and if they were trying to get an edge on me, they were in for a shock.

With Lennox's weigh-in being the Garden, I was expecting mine to be at the same venue or perhaps at the Twin Towers which were only two blocks from my hotel. When I was told it was happening on the eighth floor of what looked like a rundown school building, I was pretty surprised.

The venue was literally across the road from the hotel and would have taken about 30 seconds to walk but I was forced to get into a massive limo to get there. It took longer to jump in the car and drive round the one way system but it was all about making the big entrance.

Once inside, Junior Jones had a really small entourage whereas half of Scarborough turned up for me and took over the show. Junior had nothing to say, I had nothing to say and we were out of there in no time, it was incredibly flat. Thankfully, the night itself was about to exceed all my expectations of how incredible an evening of boxing can really be.

****

DESPITE the fact that the NYSAC had me jumping through hoops during the days leading up to this fight, I was happy and if anything a little surprised that they allowed me to come in second into the arena.

As I walked out from the tunnel with Pollard, Maloney and my brother Dean, I was expecting thousands of Americans to be shouting and possibly booing, but I was totally wrong.

Dean got so caught up in the spirit of things and the English chants that he started to join in, but not for long once Pollard had given him one of his famous looks.

As I stepped through the ropes I took a look at Jones and couldn't believe how much he'd blown up from the 12 hours before. At the weigh-in he looked very thin and drawn, almost ill. I could put on up to ten pounds after a weigh-in, but he looked almost twice that.

As the bell rang for the first round, I started to feign a lot of punches in an attempt to draw him out, so I could counter. Yet, from the opening bell, it became clear just how hard this man could hit. With a significant height and reach advantage, he didn't flick out jabs, he rammed them down my throat so hard, they almost sent me back home.

Every time he landed with his jab, it made a thudding noise which rattled my head. This was the difference between ordinary and world class punching.

Less than a minute in, I realised that I couldn't eat many more of those jabs and needed to keep my head movement constant to make sure that if he did land, it wouldn't always be flush.

I felt the first round was about even, so I decided I wanted to give the judges something to let them know I was around. I threw a hard overhand right that connected beautifully and, soon after, landed exactly the same shot. The rest of the round I did exactly as I wanted. Double hooks to the body with perfect range, making Jones miss and landing at exactly the moment I wanted to. I was on a real high.

The second I got back, Steve refocused me and told me not to get carried away. More of the same in the third and fourth and Jones was starting to complain to the ref about low blows. At one point I threw a beautiful left hook to the body and Jones looked to the ref but all he said was, 'Good shot.'

Round seven, I threw a great left hook to the head and opened a cut just under his right eyebrow. Although he fought much better in the eighth and landed much more, he was the one who walked back to the corner with blood coming from his mouth and a half-closed eye. I was feeling very confident now.

A minute into the ninth, Jones threw a big straight right that caught me flush on the chin. I'd already started to load up a punch of my own and both my feet were pretty much off the ground, so when it hit me I had no balance to do anything but hit the deck.

It wasn't a concussive punch, but certainly hard enough to put me on my backside, make me take the eight-count and remind me that I was in a fight. My head was clear, but I realised that I'd given away a 10-8 round.

Jones came out in the 10th with a lot of bravado. He was letting loose with shots and combinations that he hadn't thrown the rest of the fight and I'm sure his trainer, Teddy Atlas, had probably told him to go for the stoppage after the knock-down.

With about 20 seconds left of a round which was going his way, I caught him with a cracking left hook to the jaw which stiffened his legs immediately. For the remaining seconds left, I connected with about a dozen unanswered punches and was surprised the ref didn't step in to call it off. Jones was in plenty of trouble.

I had no intention of it going another two rounds and despite the inconsistent refereeing and my late cut, it didn't. I was now the IBO and IBF world champion. Special didn't even start to describe the occasion.

****

CATCHING up with my mates later that night was a lot of fun. I remember chatting with Neil Cox, who was sat near ringside, and asked him if it had been worth the trip.

He replied, 'I enjoyed it so much, that I almost got in trouble. When you knocked Jones down in the 11th, I was jumping up and down rooting for you, when the guy behind me yells out in a deep voice, 'Sit down. Sit down. I can't see.' I turned around and there was this huge bloke wearing a big white leather jacket – it was Sylvester Stallone!'

After a couple of beers I headed back to my hotel and left the lads to party hard – and they did. Later that night, after a few beers, my brother crashed out and the lads decided it would be fun to stick pizza up his nose, in his ears and all over his head and take a few photos for the scrapbook. When he woke up in the morning he was fuming.

Dean made sure he got his revenge the night before we flew back. Once Neil, Daz and Kenny had passed out, he broke out the Immac hair removal cream and put it on one of their eyebrows, their chest hair and part of their moustaches.

When I saw them the next morning ready to head off to the airport I dropped my cases, most people would have shaved the rest off but these guys didn't.

Neil Featherby was in uncontrollable fits of laughter every time he looked at them. Coxey was probably the funniest though. He was so deadpan about it, thinking that if he didn't mention it, nobody would notice. How they managed to get through passport control I'll never know.

When we finally did get back, Scarborough had organised yet another parade for me. Although I'm not big on being the centre of attention I could never get tired of open-top bus tours around Scarborough and the sounds of the cars beeping their horns as we made our way to the Spa balcony after winning or defending world titles.

I wasn't sure if life could get much better.

'**F**or two weeks after the fight, I could hardly sleep at all. I just wanted him to wake up. I am still worried about Ingle's condition and I sometimes spend sleepless nights over it. I wanted the title badly, but not like that.'
      - *Mbulelo Botile*, **The Times**, *2008, interview by Owen Slot*

Round 13

□

Another World

SOON after the Jones fight I was thinking about the Naz rematch and the possibility of retiring. My hands didn't have a great deal of life left in them and my aim was to have one or two more paydays to see me and my family right, then decide what to do with my time afterwards.

I would have loved to have gone straight into the Naz fight, but he already had a contest lined up with Augie Sanchez. Again, I ended up commentating for Sky at their studios in London and every time I had the chance to drop a hint to him or his team about the rematch, I would.

After stopping Sanchez in the fourth I said, 'It wasn't a bad performance, but he seemed a bit sloppy. If he's looking to challenge for my two belts, he'll need to do better than that.' I was joking about his performance as he absolutely demolished him. I was just trying to get the media to cook up some rivalry between us again.

Soon after the Sanchez win, it was rumoured that Naz had rejected offers of up to £4 million to move up to super featherweight and fight the Brazilian knockout king, Acelino

Freitas. After everything had been deducted from my purse, I was almost struggling to make five figures. It didn't seem right.

Unfortunately, I was not in the position to choose who I fought next as the IBF had told me I needed to defend against the number one contender, who was a South African boxer by the name of Mbulelo Botile. I could have done with an easier opponent straight after fighting three top world champions consecutively.

Botile had won the IBF bantamweight crown in 1995 in only his 15th fight and defended it successfully five times but, in my eyes, he was a stepping stone to Naz or another big and possible final payday. He'd not met the same calibre of boxer I had.

I never underestimated Botile. I never did that to any fellow professional.

I remember fighting Peter Buckley in my early days as a pro and many people were writing him off because he was a journeyman. I never for one second thought it would be easy. I kept telling myself, 'If this guy has been able to stay in there with 50 opponents, he has great defensive skill, knows how to slide a punch, counter and could be very dangerous if I lose concentration.'

I did the same for every fighter. The easier the fight, the more I was probably concerned about getting sucker punched or making mistakes.

I realised there was no sense in moping around and needed to get back into training. The fight was set for the 30 September, 2000 at the Ice Arena in Hull and I set up camp again at the squash courts on Filey Road, Scarborough, as they had served me very well for the Jones fight.

Unfortunately, towards the end of August, I picked up a very painful wrist injury and had to postpone the fight until November. In all honesty, it wasn't an overnight thing. I was never one for complaining about injuries, but this time I realised I needed a break to repair.

The wrist was the straw that broke the camel's back as my hands had become more and more fragile over the years through sparring, pounding the bags and pads, and landing over 100 punches per round against a number of world-class fighters.

Every time I'd make impact with my hands, it was like I was connecting with an electric shock. The pain that flew up my arm and neck was very uncomfortable.

To top it off, I also had a very painful groin injury. If it was just my hands which were injured, that wouldn't have been great, at least I could still run and move around the ring, but I couldn't do that either now.

As much as I wanted to keep focused, carrying these injuries didn't allow my workouts to be as intense and the fact is I simply wasn't burning as many calories as I needed to. It was very demoralising as I had to work like a madman to make weight normally but this made it near impossible and, in all honesty, my discipline started to slip a bit.

Don't get me wrong – I wasn't down the chippie having triple cod and chips, followed by six pints of lager – but for someone who has always been predisposed to weight gain ever since he was a kid, I was walking around at between 11 and 12 stone in a matter of weeks.

The mental frustration of weight gain whilst still training, yet knowing I couldn't train to my full potential was not putting me in the best frame of mind. I couldn't prepare how I wanted to.

Whilst sitting at home one day watching the television, I started to reflect on my whole situation and realised that my entourage had built up to something silly. I was getting paid just over £100,000 for the Botile fight and had too many people on the payroll.

By this stage, Frank Maloney had left Panix Promotions and I decided not to sign another contract with him as my manager. I still respected Frank and the influence he had in boxing and decided to keep him on board as an advisor, but I decided to manage myself.

I felt that it made sense to get my feet back on the ground and also to save some money, when there really wasn't that much of it to start with. Things had started to crack up a bit. We'd all begun to fall out at this point and as opposed to a friendly split, it was more like when the Beatles fell apart.

****

THE rescheduling gave me about three months to get myself together. Frank Maloney was insistent on me going down to Norwich with my conditioner Neil Featherby, but I decided to stay in Scarborough where I felt comfortable.

I'll put my hands up and say I had a few nights out but not in the way that some people were making out. I'd slipped off the healthy way of living for a few weeks and was not exercising as intensely as I should have been during a training camp, but in my mind I was a long way from fight night and I didn't want to be cooped in my room for six weeks before I got down to the serious training.

Sometimes I'd play five-a-side football or hang out with my mates until the early hours nursing nothing more than a soda water all night. If I did have a drink, it was never to the point where it became an issue and certainly not an addiction. Scarborough does have a drinking culture although that's not saying everybody is an alcoholic. It's a small community and when people are doing well they like to celebrate.

Despite popular belief, I was still actually very fit. My groin injury had improved a great deal and that showed when I ran the Great North Run that October in one hour and 28 minutes. However, one run is not a training camp. My overall metabolism was still much slower and my hands were still in a right state.

Then there was another rearrangement. The new date set was 16 December, 2000, one that would haunt me thereafter.

Mentally, that was hard to readjust because I'd already stripped down a load of weight at rapid speed to get ready for the November bout and had put in a number of rounds of sparring. To have to do that all again was simply soul-destroying.

When you train by the old-fashioned methods in a nonstop camp, as I'd done for my previous title fights, it's brutal, but it works. Letting your trainer break your heart during it makes you stronger and fitter but stopping and starting three times and carrying injuries was unfamiliar territory for me. I didn't have time on my side and despite the use of supplements to burn fat, I was still overweight.

When your body needs about 4,500 calories per day but you are looking to survive on about 1,100, you still need to make sure you have enough energy to train and fluid to keep you hydrated. Neil Featherby expressed his concerns on a number of occasions about the amount of weight I needed to lose in the time I had left.

From previous camps, I knew if I was 14 lbs overweight I would need about two months to get back down. Exercise with sensible eating and fluid intake is how you do it, but over time. Time is one thing I didn't have.

The Yorkshire Hunter

I decided to turn to the controversial cabbage soup diet for two weeks, which I'd done once before, for the Michael Alldis fight. It is often used for patients with heart problems who are carrying too much weight. It allows them to lose it rapidly and still to take on nutrients.

I used to make mine up from cabbage, onion, tinned tomatoes, onion stock and a couple of peppers. I didn't like it chunky, so I'd liquidise it and then drink it from a mug. As controversial as it was, I lost about ten pounds in seven days.

I could still have main meals and other foods although one major downside was what it did with my guts. Apart from my breath being deadly, you didn't want to be standing near me once I started digesting.

With about three weeks to go before fight night, I started to step up my sparring. I brought in partners who pushed me to my limit and also tested my fitness. In my eyes, I thought I was doing ok. I was aware that my punch count was way down and I was getting caught more often than normally but I just put it down to being a little tired and low on energy.

On one occasion Steve Pollard was furious with me. After stepping out of the ring, he said, 'Are you alright? These lads are tough, but they are ordinary Joe's. You should be playing with them and doing as you want. You don't seem right. What have you eaten today?'

When I told him just a peach, he flipped.

He went on, 'I want no part of this. If you don't eat, we are pulling the fight. The way you currently are, you'll be able to box but not at world title level.' Neil Featherby had also expressed similar concerns that same afternoon. To top it off, my mum had also attended the sparring session and she thought I was getting beaten up and had to leave.

About 9.30 that same night I called Steve up from an

Italian restaurant in Scarborough which he was familiar with and I told him I was eating a proper dinner. Steve asked me to put the restaurant owner on the phone to confirm this, just to make sure I wasn't lying, which I wasn't very good at anyway.

The owner explained that I was having a nice plate of pasta but Steve asked to speak to one of the other waiters, just to make sure I hadn't told the owner what to say in advance. Thankfully, he was satisfied and we were back on talking terms again.

The reality is that I was struggling with the weight, but I also realised that starving myself wasn't going to help. The pressure of making weight, being healthy, staying fit, preparing myself technically, getting in to the sparring, was all starting to pile up.

To make things worse, there was a rumour going round that if I didn't take the fight I'd have to fight Botile in South Africa on his terms.

For the first time in my life, I'll put my hands up and say, I wasn't prepared for the fight – and that's not just hindsight. In an ideal world I would have preferred to postpone it again because I was never ready. As it had been rescheduled a number of times, it became near impossible to cancel.

It was either fight or resign the belts. The training had got to me, the injuries had got to me and the rescheduling had got to me. My mind and body were not in great shape and I was pushing them beyond safety. I should have never have taken the fight.

****

I USED to play five-a-side everything Thursday with my mates but the closer this fight got, I stopped playing outfield to avoid getting an injury and started going in goal.

The Yorkshire Hunter

The Thursday before fight night I turned up and the second I arrived, Daz Smith said to me, 'Mate – you look grey. Everything ok?'

I said, 'Everything's fine Daz. I'll leave you some tickets on the door for Saturday and there will be a big party back at the hotel afterwards.'

That party never happened though.

The day after was the weigh-in. Although I still couldn't see it, many of the fans, like Daz, could sense something was not right with me and, as I walked in, there was a really subdued atmosphere. That was the first and only time my fans had been quiet.

I came in half-a-pound under the nine stone limit, whereas Botile came in a pound-and-a-half under, which was no real surprise as he was naturally a bantamweight.

After coming off the scales, I walked over to Glenn McCrory and Ian Darke. Glenn had covered every one of my pro fights for Sky, but looked sad because he'd been to a funeral earlier, as his 16-year-old nephew had died after a tragic battle with cancer. I'd assumed that's why he looked somewhat shocked when I went over and shook his hand.

After offering my sympathies I walked away, but I could see him chatting to Ian and shaking his head and then looking back at me. I didn't think anything of it.

On the morning of the fight, I picked up a newspaper and was happy to see I was a 6-1 favourite. I'd watched videos with Steve Pollard of Botile's fights and we'd worked out that he was a fairly predictable come-forward fighter with not a great deal of side-to-side movement.

My style was perfect to dismantle him. We'd worked out that with my speed, workrate and movement, Botile would never be able to get in range. Unfortunately, the version of Paul Ingle who was capable of that did not show up that night.

The way I'd felt in my training camps when I fought Naz, Medina or Junior Jones was at another level. In my current condition, I wouldn't have lasted three rounds with any of those guys. The way I looked for this fight, it was as if I'd never fought before.

From the opening bell, I lacked spark. I have always been known to bounce around on my feet from the time I come out of the tunnel, to when the final bell rings, but I didn't that night. I was bouncing, but it was like I had lead boots on. There was someone who looked like me in there, but it wasn't me.

The very first punch Botile threw in the first round caught me flush. The old Paul Ingle would have slipped that easily and probably countered with a two or three punch combination. I wasn't able to find my rhythm, there was no snap in my punches and everything I threw was out of range.

Halfway through that round he caught me with a left hook which almost had me on the floor. The only part of my game which remained unaffected was my heart. I refused to give up, even though I was taking a hell of a battering.

After being knocked down in the last ten seconds of the 11th, I came back to the corner for the final round. Steve said to me, 'Are you alright?'

I replied, 'I'm ok, but I know I've got to knock him out.'

Frank Maloney then asked me, 'You ok, Paul?'

I turned to him and said, 'I'm alright, Frank.'

My face was a mess. I was bloodied, swollen and had nothing left in the tank. Within a matter of seconds of the bell ringing for the final round, I was on the canvas again and the ref was over me counting.

Within a couple of minutes my eyes were closed and I faded out of consciousness.

'A scientist called JS Haldane stated many years ago: 'A lack of oxygen not only stops the machine it wrecks the machinery.' That is why the golden hour is so important.'
- Robert Battersby, Paul Ingle's neurosurgeon

Round 14

☐

Through My Mother's Eyes

THE injury from the Botile fight left me with pretty much no memory of the days, weeks and months afterwards.

For me to write what happened during this time would be inaccurate because it would be second-hand information as I was out cold most of that time. It only seems appropriate that you feel the emotion and pain of what happened to me through somebody who never left my side after the fight and who never gave up on me – my mum.

****

THE night before the fight, Paul called me saying he had a headache. He thought it might be the air conditioning in the hotel, so I told him to go for a walk to clear his head. He sounded ok though.

The 16th December, 2000 started off as a normal day. I'd been out doing a bit of Christmas shopping in Scarborough town centre and got home late afternoon to have my tea. I never used to turn on the television when Paul fought, only once I knew the fight was over. On this evening, like so many others, I was waiting for him to call to say he'd won again. I'm not huge into boxing but I did know the lad he was fighting was nowhere near as good as Naz, Medina or Jones, so I was confident he would be ringing anytime soon.

Finally the phone rung – but it wasn't Paul. It was my sister-in-law calling to say he'd been knocked down and the doctors were in the ring. She said she'd phone back with more details as soon as she had them. My heart instantly skipped.

As I came off the phone, I turned the television on. I was on my own and crying my eyes out. It was a horrible feeling, as if I'd jumped into freezing cold water. I was shocked, shivering and found it difficult to speak.

The phone then went again. My sister-in-law said, 'He's been rushed to Northern General Hospital in Sheffield. They think he has a bleed, but don't worry about it.'

I knew she was trying to keep me calm, but the worst thing you can say to anyone when they have just been told news like this is too keep calm and not worry.

The phone started ringing off the hook from people wanting to help or give updates. There were some deadly silences during the conversations and I could feel my heart pounding hard.

About five minutes later, my brothers and sisters started coming to the house. That was a massive help because I'd never felt so lonely in my life.

My brother Pete had been watching the fight down the road at the pub and could see I was in a right state.

Mercifully, he knew I'd respond to straight talking and said, 'You need to get in that car. This is the time he needs you most. We'll all head off soon, but you need to be on your way – now.'

A minute later I opened the door to let my sister in and noticed that outside was mobbed with journalists and photographers trying to get a photo or an interview with me.

Scarborough only has a population of about 50,000 people and there's not many who weren't either at the fight or watching it on the television.

Paul was regarded by many as a local sporting hero and a lot were acting as if he'd died already. It was the worst moment of my life and I hadn't even seen him by this stage.

My sister took care of it and updated them with what little she knew and asked them to respectfully leave, as I didn't want to speak to anyone - I just wanted to be at the hospital. I was in no mood or condition to say anything rational.

A friend of mine then came round and asked if I wanted a lift. I was numb and accepted it gratefully.

The two hour journey to the hospital seemed to take forever. I don't remember saying a word the entire time.

****

AS we pulled up to the Royal Hallamshire Hospital, there were journalists, photographers, press vans and lorries, with massive satellite dishes on top, all congregating. This was no longer a headline for the locals in Scarborough, it was worldwide news which was spreading like wildfire.

We sprinted to reception and ignored all the journalists who instantly spotted us and came running over with microphones and cameras.

On arriving at reception, I got escorted by security to the lift and then Paul's room. Thankfully they didn't allow the press gang to follow us and also had guards outside the ward to make sure nobody tried to sneak in to get a quick photo.

As we reached Paul's floor and the lift doors opened, there were loads of people waiting outside, including Rocky Rowe and Franny Norton, a jockey and good friend of Paul's, but it was all a blur to me.

Spencer Oliver, who'd had a blood clot removed the year before, was one of the first people to arrive at the hospital to see Paul and the moment he saw me, he walked straight up to me, gave me a hug and said, 'I'm living proof that he can come through this. Yes it's bad and the hours ahead are crucial, but he's from the same mould as me. He's a fighter.' I'll never forget those words, it was an enormous help and I'm still extremely grateful to him.

Within minutes of arriving, Paul passed me on the operating trolley – he'd just come out of theatre. It was one of the most spine-chilling moments of my life. I just froze, I couldn't even cry.

I asked the nurse if I could go with him and she said, 'Give us a few minutes to set him up.' About 15 minutes later I was allowed to go into his room, by which point the doctors and nurses had put around 20 tubes in him, which were all connected to the beeping machines.

Before stepping into the intensive care room, I thought I would be a nervous wreck, but the moment I opened the door, he looked so peaceful, which somehow made me very calm. I must have been in shock, as the sight of Paul with all the tubes coming out of him, his head covered in bandages and the ventilator helping him breathe had no effect on me.

I was told that I could talk to Paul but whether or not he could hear was another story. So I sat next to him, held his hand and started to chat to him.

A few minutes later, a nurse took us to a private office where the neurosurgeon, Robert Battersby, updated me on the operation he'd done and Paul's condition at that point. When I opened the door, Paul's girlfriend was there along with Frank Maloney and Steve Pollard. Everybody was very, very upset. It was awful.

Next thing, Mr Battersby walked through the door and, before he was even seated, I asked him desperately, 'The press has been saying a lot of stuff. I know they like to grab the headlines. I just need to know how much of it is true.'

Mr Battersby was a true professional and a warm man but he kept himself detached enough to not get emotionally involved with Paul. He didn't lead us up the garden path telling us Paul was fine, but in the same breath he didn't tell us he was on death's door.

He was also very aware that any comments could spread like wildfire and easily end up on the front page of a tabloid. Unfortunately, some of the press did twist the headlines to sell papers over the coming weeks, but Mr Battersby gave us a balanced view of the positives and negatives.

There was talk that Paul had been taken to the wrong hospital, but this wasn't the case. Mr Battersby explained the system to us, 'Whenever there's a bad head injury, the patient is taken to a casualty department to be resuscitated.'

He went on, 'There were two big hospitals in Sheffield – the Royal Hallamshire Hospital and the Northern General Hospital, the latter being the closer to the fight venue, so that's why Paul was taken there first for resuscitation. He was then moved for the operation.'

I continued to ask Mr Battersby more questions.

'I keep hearing people say, 'Thank God he was operated in the golden hour.' What's the golden hour?'

He calmly went on to explain. 'The most important factor is that the brain gets oxygen. Nothing else matters. The brain requires oxygen and glucose to survive. Those are the two primary requirements.

'If a person is deprived of oxygen for about three minutes, most will recover. If the time is five minutes, about half will recover. If that time is ten minutes, none will recover.'

What had happened during those two hours whilst I was in a car travelling to the hospital was incredible, shocking and emotionally wrecking, but I still needed to find out the whole story in greater detail.

****

THROUGH chatting with those present at the boxing and those involved with saving and operating on him, I was able to piece together exactly what had happened before I arrived at the hospital.

Problems started to occur soon after Paul collapsed, however, the main damage had already been done in the 12 rounds he'd just fought. As with other boxers who had suffered brain injuries, during the fight, even if the brain is swollen, there's very little which will show it. Although he had a heavy nosebleed during the fight, it was not related. He got that by being hit on the nose – nothing more than that.

When Paul collapsed, he was placed flat on his back, which was very strange, as there were concerns he might have broken his neck. From what I can understand, though, the chances of a boxer breaking their neck in the ring is very low.

As Mr Battersby would go on to say at a later stage, 'If you are unconscious and face heaven that's where you're going.' Paul should have been put in the recovery position, especially as his pasta meal was going to be vomited up several times over the next 30 minutes. Vomit when you are unconscious is a killer because it goes straight into your lungs.

The medical staff ringside, were simply not trained to deal with something like this. What actually needed doing was pretty simple. A person with the correct medical knowledge, would have turned Paul on his side and put a tube down his throat and pulled his tongue forward so he could breathe properly. Unfortunately, this didn't happen and it caused plenty of problems.

Soon after collapsing in the ring, Paul was whisked off to the Northern General by private ambulance. He had vomited during the journey. When he arrived, his Glasgow Coma Score was at three, the lowest possible score, which meant he was in a deep coma. His eyes were not responding normally and his pupils were dilating.

He was unable to speak or move and he was totally unresponsive, which meant he probably felt no pain. In this situation, these readings are often referred to as coroner's signs, when the doctor would normally expect the patient's outcome to be so poor that they would usually die and need to be referred to the coroner. Paul was in plenty of trouble.

The first thing they did when Paul arrived was to put a tube down his throat to give him a clear airway. Then they put him on a breathing machine, before suctioning his lungs.

After sorting out his breathing, they gave him a CT brain scan, which showed a clot about the size of a one centimetre sliver of liver on the inside of his skull. His brain was also swelling as a reaction to having the clot, so he was given something called Mannitol, a dehydrating drug.

It makes you pee gallons but shrinks the brain down. It bought Paul about 20-30 minutes and he was transferred straight away to the Royal Hallamshire, where they had a neurosurgical unit.

Paul arrived at the Northern at 10.55pm straight from the boxing arena and by 11:40pm he was ready to be operated on. Having the tube down his throat and the Mannitol had basically saved his life, as his pulse and blood pressure had almost come back to normal levels.

Mr Battersby's role in Paul's operation was key but the only reason he was present to carry it out was because of someone else's misfortune.

At the precise moment Paul collapsed and had been taken to the Northern General, Mr Battersby was at home and had been waiting for confirmation of another man, with a similar injury, who had been in a car accident.

At this point, Mr Battersby was set to remain at home as there was a junior doctor on site who was trained to deal with this kind of emergency. I would have thought that brain surgery of any kind would have been very complex, but apparently it's not.

Don't get me wrong, it's a very delicate operation, but for those with the correct neurosurgical training, it's usually fairly quick and relatively straightforward, unless there are complications. It's the management afterwards which can be difficult and that's where the neurosurgical team on the intensive care unit are so important.

Whilst waiting for an update of the car accident patient, Mr Battersby received a call saying, 'We've got a boxer on the way' and he decided that he had best go in.

Since starting neurosurgery in 1975, Mr Battersby had dealt with only minor head injuries in boxers, but never a major one like Paul's. He had operated on many similar blood clots to Paul's, which normally occur after car accidents and other severe injuries such as falls from buildings.

Dressed in jeans and a T-shirt, he pulled up in his beat -up old Vauxhall Astra, which was probably a good thing as he managed to walk past the media without them having a clue as to who he was. I'm sure they would have given anything at that point to have a few words from him.

The problem then arose that they only had one emergency theatre ready at the Royal Hallamshire, so they had to open up another and get more emergency staff for both patients to be operated on at the same time, just in case there was an overlap.

The move was a wise one as both Paul and the other guy turned up at exactly the same time. Both were taken down to theatre, both with identical head injuries, both as serious as each other.

When Paul arrived, the anaesthetist was very concerned as Paul kept getting pasta coming up through his tube. He would have suffered a lack of oxygen to the brain as a result and it was also contributing to the brain swelling.

With time crucial, Mr Battersby went to work on the blood clot pressing on Paul's brain. First thing he did, was to make a large cut in the skin on the right side of his head and then peel the layer of scalp back, to reveal the skull on that side. He then made a series of holes with a hand drill, before connecting them using a hand-operated Gigli saw, which looks like a serrated cheese wire, to remove the skull plate. The piece of bone removed was as large as your outstretched hand.

If you think about the brain as a mushroom with a stalk, if you twist it, the stalk stays still, but the brain rotates around. In between the skull lining and the brain are many delicate veins, which if you twist the brain suddenly, these veins will tear. That's what caused Paul's bleeding.

The blood started to spread around the space between the brain and the skull and that's how Paul's clot built up. Once the bone has been lifted away, you can relax a bit because some of the pressure is off the brain, but you still have to be quick because the brain then starts to swell up.

The clot was then removed gently, by sucking it out and slowly flushing the area with a saline solution.

This was the most crucial part of the operation, as it was essential that Mr Battersby did not damage the surface of the brain. His next job was to find the ruptured vein which had formed the clot and stop the bleeding. Everything that was being done was being done with precision, but also great urgency.

Unlike most other parts of the body, you can't always cauterise a vein satisfactorily in the brain to stop it bleeding because it's too delicate, so they use a mesh similar to a cobweb. After making sure all the bleeding has stopped the layers are gently replaced and the scalp sewn back up. The piece of skull is left out at this stage to allow the injured brain to swell, which is going to happen just like your ankle swells after you twist it.

The operation took about two and a half hours. The raw truth was that Paul's chances of survival were 50/50. The next 72 hours were crucial in terms of him pulling through.

Had Paul not been unconscious at the end of the 12th round of the Botile fight and managed to get back to his room and fall asleep, he would have certainly died. That's perhaps the only bit of luck he had that night.

****

MY conversations with Mr Battersby in those first few hours were very frequent, but also very difficult to deal with. Every time me and Paul's girlfriend would go to his room for an update, I'd come out a mess.

In the end, I couldn't bring myself to go there because

every time he would call us he had more bad news. Paul's girlfriend had to go in and get updates for me.

On top of all this, every time I stepped out into the corridor, Paul's friends, family and people from the boxing world were all talking about why he collapsed and hearing words like, 'weight loss.' Reasons as to why he shouldn't have been in the ring was not what I needed. People were also throwing blame at each other which again didn't help. It was a nightmare.

I'd been there a few hours when the sun had started to rise. The corridor was littered with Paul's close friends such as Rocky Rowe and Kenny Brock who had decided to sleep there overnight. My sense of time had gone out of the window. It was like being hungover and having a high fever all in one. You kind of know where you are, but you keep drifting in and out in terms of where you think you are.

A great number of people who were at the fight had gone home thinking Paul was going to be ok and many others simply didn't want to crowd the ward, especially as no news was known straight after the fight but soon appeared in the morning as word spread very quickly about Paul's condition.

Paul's brother Dean arrived about 7am, around the same time as a couple of my brothers.

My brother Andrew walked over and said, 'We all got back on the bus last night and like most of the people thought he'd been taken to hospital as a precaution, just to get checked over. Then half way home I got a phone call from Jen [our sister] saying, 'He's in a really bad way.'

Dean took it very badly when he walked in to see Paul. He almost collapsed and had to be helped out of the room.

These were very distressing times. I got us a cup of

tea, sat down with him and decided that talking about what happened the night before might help him get it off his chest.

'It was awful mam. Chris Tate from *Emmerdale* [actor Peter Amory] was sitting behind me and he was shouting to the ref to stop it. It was like I was in a daze. I was numb. People were speaking to me, but I couldn't reply.

'When Paul went down and was laid out, I remember pushing people out of the way to get to him and being pinned back by the security guards. Neil Featherby was trying to stop the guards from holding me and people from the seats at the back were running forward to see what was going on.

'Everyone was still loudly chanting his name. It was pandemonium but all in slow motion. I remember the ambulance setting off and I jumped in somebody's car. I was running around the hospital frantically and then seeing Paul in a room with loads of people inside and Paul looking a state. Frank Maloney pulled me out and said, "Stay out of there. It's not going to do you any good." I was stuck in a car home soon after and sat with my head in my hands all the way home, really upset. It's awful mam.'

Wayne Smith arrived soon after Dean. I'd known Wayne since he was a nipper and he was very close to Paul and the Ingle family. As he walked in, he gave me a big hug and we were both very emotional.

He then cracked a joke which lightened the mood for a second. 'Even when Paul is unconscious, he's still able to wind us up. Last night everyone was calling me up to find out the latest and I didn't know anything.

'I decided to call his mobile and, after a few rings, Paul answers. 'Hello. One second please. Go on. Sorry – Just a second. Hello, hello – can you hear me?' Then the beep started. It was his wind-up voicemail. I wish it wasn't though Carol. I wish he was winding me up in person right now.'

We both became emotional again.

Wayne then walked over to Dean and my brothers, who all had their heads down.

Wayne asked, 'What's the latest?'

Dean replied, 'He's lying there motionless, tubes hanging out of him, monitors all around him making noises. Go and take a look at him. He's in that room.'

The nurse would always check with me who was allowed to go inside so I gave her the nod and said, 'He's like family.'

I could hear Wayne talking to Paul and then shouting, 'Paul – can you hear me? Wake up Paul. Wake up.'

Wayne found it very tough to accept but for the coming weeks, every day he had off work, without fail he'd drive up to Sheffield to see him. Like all of Paul's true mates, he never gave up on him and never would.

A little later that morning, another good friend of Paul's and ex-sparring partner Mark Legge turned up. He'd spent the night just down the road in Hillsborough to be close to Paul and would, in fact, end up booking into a bed and breakfast for the next month.

Mark asked me how he was doing. I told him, 'His chances of pulling through were very slim straight after the operation, but he seems slightly better now. Still pretty bad though.'

Mark then said, 'If you give Paul a one per cent chance, he will take it and make it work being the character he is. He'll come through Carol.'

He then went on to tell me a story. 'Years ago, me and Paul had a chat about a day like this happening. I said to him that I'd prefer it would happen to me rather than him as I'd never want to see him get hurt. Neither of us thought this day would happen.'

Mark paused a bit and then said, 'I would give anything to swap places with him right now.'

I replied, 'You're here now Mark. That's all that counts. Paul wouldn't want you in there. He needs you out here.'

Phone calls started coming in thick and fast. Everyone from the likes of Peter Richardson through to John Amos, who said, 'Hardly anybody has slept on the Edgehill estate last night. Everybody's been stuck to their televisions and radios waiting for updates. They all want Paul back on his feet. I want Paul back on his feet.'

As if Paul's condition wasn't bad enough, I couldn't believe how low some people could be. Journalists kept coming up to me in the hospital, wanting to get a photo of Paul. There was a guy from the *News of The World* sat in the lobby of the hospital waiting for us. It was very uncomfortable. Apart from the fact it was terrible timing, I couldn't have done an interview if I had tried at that point. I wanted my son to get better – I didn't want a microphone in my face.

This guy was so persistent to get a story. He said, 'I need a story and I'm not leaving.'

I turned to him and shouted, 'My son's on his deathbed here and you need a story!' Instead of leaving, he just sat there hoping I might say something later or he might get a glimpse of Paul. He was lowlife scum.

They didn't give up though. The lengths they went to was disgusting. Wearing disguises and even pretending to be doctors and nurses to get close. At one point Dean could see I was getting upset and jumped in. He grabbed this guy by the collar and threw him back into the lift.

The journalist started to complain. I would normally have been angry at Dean for that kind of behaviour but instead, as he sat down next to me and put his arm around me, I said, 'Thanks Dean. Your brother would be proud.'

As the evening drew close, Frank Maloney told me, 'You need to get some sleep and have a meal, you'll be no good to anyone otherwise. I've arranged for you to stay at the hotel, in Paul's room. It's only 10 minutes away so we can be back very quickly whenever you decide to return.' Although I didn't want to leave, I knew it made sense to get out of the ward for a few hours.

I went back with Frank and we headed straight to the bar area to order food. There was a room full of long and sad faces including Paul's cut man Mick Williamson, Neil Featherby, Peter Amory and many more. Hardly anyone was speaking and when they did it was quick softly spoken sentences. Everyone was numb.

After eating, I went back to Paul's room to try and get some sleep. It just didn't feel right seeing Paul's clothes and bags on the floor and, when I looked out of the window, I saw his car in the car park. That set me off again.

As much as I tried, I couldn't get a wink of sleep. That beeping sound from the monitors and machines in Paul's room was still ringing in my ears and I just couldn't stay in that room knowing my boy was in that hospital. Within a couple of hours of arriving at the hotel, I was back at Paul's bedside again.

The place was already becoming too familiar for my liking. Up to this point in my life, I'd only ever really been to hospital when my dad had a stroke and I wasn't there long enough to take in the smells, colours and feel for the place.

Paul had always been as fit as a fiddle. Apart from having his appendix out, he was never in hospital. After all his fights, he never needed to visit one afterwards, because he was never in any real trouble.

When I arrived back, Kenny Brock and Rocky Rowe were sleeping outside Paul's room. I let them carry on but, as with everyone, later acknowledged the incredible support they were giving my son.

By the morning of the 18th of December, I realised that I needed to go home to get some fresh clothes and collect a few other bits. With everything that had gone on in the last 48 hours, I'd totally forgotten it was my 50th birthday. When I got to the house, my brothers and sisters were there with cards and presents but it was all very subdued.

Then I spotted a huge bunch of beautiful red roses and started walking across to them. My brothers and sisters went silent as they looked at me and a few of them started to cry.

As a surprise, Paul had arranged for 50 red roses and also a big meal for the whole family before the accident. As I started to read the card, I broke down uncontrollably. I kept one of the roses and pressed it in a book, which I still have to this day.

As I started to pull myself together, I suddenly noticed something incredible. The number of 'Get well soon' cards and messages that had arrived were immense and the number of flowers which other boxers, friends and family had sent, totally filled up my kitchen and most of the lounge.

In addition, lovely emails had started to come in from abroad, including the likes of Joe Cortez and fellow world champions such as Lennox Lewis and European champ Wayne Alexander.

His old opponent Junior Jones also had some lovely words to say. 'I'm shocked, surprised and can't believe it's happened to him. The same guy who was in the ring with me and beaten me less than a year ago.

'He was such a good fighter and I'm very, very shocked. I'm finding this difficult to discuss with anyone else at the moment as I haven't come to terms with it myself yet.

I'm going to pray he makes a full recovery. I want to hear he's woken up and is talking fine.'

At a time where I needed something positive, this was a nice step in the right direction.

I thought to myself, 'If you were here Paul, you'd love this. When you wake up I'm going to tell you all about it. Please wake up Paul. Please.'

Through My Mother's Eyes

'**Y**ou can't fight anymore,
Paul. That's it in the
ring. It's over.'
- Senior doctor,
Castle Hill Hospital, 2001

Round 15

□

Coming Round

(Carol Ingle continues to narrate)

THE operation was the easy part up to this point. It was the problems that started to develop afterwards that made Paul's condition vulnerable.

Due to his lung being full of pasta, it collapsed and he went on to develop pneumonia. He also contracted something called hypernatremia, which was something else that could prove fatal.

Anaemia also got thrown into the mix, which didn't make much sense, because he hadn't lost a lot of blood. Apparently he was bleeding somehow as his body's reaction to blood clotting had gone haywire. Over the next few days, Paul needed a couple of transfusions. How much more could he take?

By the third day it was quite obvious that Paul wasn't going to just wake up and all would be back to normal. As a result of the lung infection, he needed a tracheotomy to get him breathing correctly. Although this helped to get the

209

collapsed lung working again, he was still as close to dying as he was to living.

Paul was now being slowly brought out of his induced coma. Soon after, he started having fits, which was yet another horrible effect. It happened more times over the next few days and Paul ended up needing to go on medication for epilepsy for a year.

I was told that it could contribute to Paul putting on a lot of weight over time but at this point I couldn't have cared less as it wasn't certain whether he'd make it out of the hospital alive by the end of the week.

Later that day, Mr Battersby said, 'If it hadn't been for Paul's incredible level of fitness as a boxer, he would probably have died.'

Although I was happy that he'd cheated death, it was heartbreaking for a mother to have to see a machine breathing for her son, with a tube coming out of his throat. I can still hear the sound of that machine and see his lungs going up and down in a forced manner.

By day five, Paul started to show some encouraging signs such as moving his arms and legs, although most of the movement was coming from the left side of his body. He then started to open his eyes on and off, which was a major step forward for me.

Although we'd been talking to him up to that point, we all really started to put some effort into snapping him out of the coma.

The next few weeks were full of more scares and death-defying moments. The chest infection was still a major problem and they had to put him on several courses of heavy duty antibiotics as well as having loads of physio.

The days ticked by and I was unaware if it was Sunday or Thursday. My day started and finished in that matchbox room which Paul was in and I wasn't leaving until I saw some major signs of progress.

One day, just as I was walking out of the room to go to the canteen and get a tea, a nurse wished me merry Christmas and then walked off. I looked at her strangely and then carried on walking. It wasn't until I saw a family walking in with presents for another patient that I suddenly realised it was Christmas Day.

We had been due to have Christmas dinner at my sister Jen's but instead, me and Dean were sitting in a hospital canteen, without appetite, pushing the food around our plates. Christmas Day came and went just like any other at the hospital but Boxing Day had a nice little surprise.

It was now ten days since the accident and Paul had been moved from intensive care to another room. We had been down to the shop to get a newspaper and were just getting back into the lift, when Dean said with a surprised look on his face, 'That's Naz over there.' I assured him it wasn't and we went back to Paul's bedside.

Next thing, the nurse comes into the room and says, 'Can Paul have a visitor? It's Prince Naseem.' Dean was right.

I'd never met him before, so we introduced ourselves and Naz explained that he'd been in Mecca saying prayers and got there as soon as he could. Although it was a total coincidence, it was appropriate that it was Boxing Day for Naz to be there.

They very respectfully shook our hands and then welled up with tears as they walked over to Paul's bedside. Although Paul was coming in and out of consciousness at this stage, he hadn't spoken yet and was still heavily sedated.

Naz and his brother stood either side of Paul and each held one of his hands, before saying a prayer in Arabic. Naz then looked at Paul, as if he were totally awake and with a tear in his eye started saying to him, 'We are going to walk out of this hospital together. I'm going to keep coming back and we're going to walk out of this hospital together. I want to win that title back for you.'

He stayed for about an hour, which was much longer than many could take.

****

AS if having a collapsed lung wasn't enough, Paul's liver started to pack up and the doctors weren't sure why. They carried out loads of tests and at first thought it might have been something to do with the tablets he was taking for his fits.

In the end it was the brain injury which was causing the problem. Mr Battersby explained, 'Your liver is in charge of processing the glucose needed. When you've had a brain injury, it stops working.' I'm not sure what he and his team did in the days which followed, but they got his liver working again and, within a matter of days, Paul had pulled through that scare.

Soon after the two-week mark, I was in his room with Steve Pollard and Paul's girlfriend and we were just staring at him. The only noise you could hear were the machines. Suddenly, Paul did the thing we'd all been waiting for – he came to and spoke.

Most people think, when somebody wakes from a coma it's like they do in the Hollywood movies. It doesn't happen that way in real life. He opened his eyes, saw me and said, 'Hiya mam,' and then went straight back to being unconscious again. It was a very emotional moment and we all broke down in tears.

Regaining full consciousness is a gradual process. It

took Paul the next three months. The waking up and falling back into unconsciousness became more and more frequent, although there were a few tense moments when he'd wake up in a panic and try to pull out all his tubes.

The day after first snapping out of the coma, they sat Paul in a chair. He looked like a rag doll that had been thrown in the corner. He had no strength in him, his head was down on his chin and his leg was jerking.

His fighting weight was nine stone but he was now about seven, had legs like sparrows and was being fed through drips and tubes. He was so thin it was heartbreaking.

I remember Daz Smith coming to visit Paul on that day and he'd also brought up one of my brothers. Although he didn't say much, I knew he was torn up seeing Paul strapped to this chair.

A few minutes later, Mr Battersby came in to do a check-up and Paul unexpectedly turned on the charm and got us in good spirits. Mr Battersby asked him, 'Do you remember me?' Paul looked at him, looked at Daz, then looked back and said, 'You're the guy off *Coronation Street*.'

Whether or not Paul was joking didn't matter. He did something we hadn't done in weeks – laugh. We were all laughing so hard, our bellies were fit to burst.

****

A FEW days after first waking up, Mr Battersby told us that Paul had lost part of his sight in his left eye. Even with laser and all the technology around, there was nothing that could be done. The problem was not with the eye itself, it was the part of the brain connected to the eye. Yet another unexpected surprise.

But there was more to come.

Paul had also been diagnosed with a hernia, but he wasn't able to have it operated on straight away as he'd contracted an infection at the hospital. At the time, MRSA was all over the television as the killer bug, so I asked, 'It's not that MRSA bug is it?' But it was. It just seemed like he couldn't get a break.

The MRSA would take nine months and several doses of antibiotics to get rid of before Paul finally had that op.

Six weeks after the night of the fight, Paul was taken to a rehabilitation centre called Castle Hill, which was about 40 miles away from home in Hull. As he started to regain consciousness more and more, the doctors started putting Paul through some basic tests to see how he was working physically.

Paul's right arm was very weak and that's when they broke the news to us that he had suffered a stroke as a result of the injury. How badly it had affected him at this point was hard to say. I instantly started to panic wondering what else was going to surface.

Soon after, they got to work on giving Paul physiotherapy, most of which I wasn't present for because there was a good chance I'd get upset when I saw him struggle. So I decided to do some exercises with just me and him.

I was told that he would benefit from as much light movement as he could get at this point, so I started to massage him every day to help get his blood flowing and his muscles working. I also started to shave him and keep him presentable as Paul would have hated to look like a tramp.

It's amazing how quickly muscle can waste away and I couldn't believe how much his lateral muscles had faded. When he was boxing, they were like steel. He'd throw his left hook in with serious power with them but now he was struggling just to raise his arms. In an attempt to build them up again, we used to throw a big ball for him to catch and also help with his reflexes.

The first time he stood up, it took two doctors and two nurses to steady him on his feet. I had to walk out – I couldn't see him like that.

Over the next three to four weeks, the doctors and occupational therapist carried out loads of tests to see how badly his brain had been injured. There were issues with his speech, including something called dysphasia, which basically meant he had difficulty identifying the word he wanted to use.

They also wanted to test how badly his memory had been affected. Remembering less than an hour before the accident was considered as minor, between an hour and a day was moderate, more than 24 hours to a week was considered severe and over a week extremely severe.

Paul had an extremely severe brain injury and there was a strong chance that his short-term memory might also be affected for the rest of his life. The occupational therapist used a scale to determine Paul's functionality and he was only 22 per cent of what a person should be at that point.

The other thing which happened very quickly was his weight gain. He'd gone to over ten stone and rising in about six weeks, which would also be a real problem in the future. I'd gone beyond despair by this stage. When a new issue came up, I had no option but to just deal with it and be strong for him.

Although he still couldn't walk and was in a wheelchair, the staff never gave up on him. They continued to make him stand and got him to do exercises as often as they could. Within a few days, they started walking him around the gardens. As tough as it was to watch I was also starting to feel hope. I could see that he was getting a bit better.

We then hit another minor hurdle. Paul never liked taking medicines, not even vitamin tablets when he was boxing if he could help it. If he had a pain, he preferred to see it through than take a Paracetemol or an Ibuprofen. When they brought his tablets round, he refused to take them.

He said, 'Mam, they're poisoning me.' We had to explain why he was taking them but it was no good. He didn't know where he was or what he was doing. For the moments he was conscious, as far as he knew, he'd had an accident, but he was still the champion of the world and would be back in the gym very soon.

Every time he'd wake, he would repeat exactly the same conversation again and again. I was convinced that his memory had completely gone. However, he then started to prove us wrong.

Paul's memory was certainly badly shot at this stage, but what was interesting was how his brain was piecing certain bits of information together to try and make sense. As he started to regain regular consciousness, his good friends and family started to come round and chat with him, which was exactly what Paul needed to get his brain stimulated again.

One day, our neighbour and lifelong family friend John Amos dropped round to the hospital. Paul was in bed but recognised John straight away, which was very encouraging. Paul then said, 'Johnny's horse is running today in the Grand National.'

I said, 'He hasn't got a horse, Paul.'

He replied, 'Of course he's got a horse, mam. He keeps it in the house in that stable doesn't he? Anyway, it's running this afternoon and I want to put a tenner on it to win.'

I looked at John and he smiled knowing why Paul

had said this, but didn't let on in front of him. In the meantime, me and John chose a horse from the newspaper just to keep him happy and we put a tenner on it to win.

John then explained to me outside the room what he thought Paul was thinking about. He told me, 'In my house, I've got a shower and to get into it you have to open these split doors. You open the top half and then the bottom. That's where the stable comes from.'

The nag we'd chosen went on to win at 20-1.

In the coming weeks, more and more people came to see Paul. Kenny Brock, his cousin Leanne, Daz Smith, Mark Legge and I almost had the same speech rehearsed before they went into his room.

'He's probably not going to remember you. It's not personal, it's just that his memory is shot.' However, he did remember them. Anyone who meant something to him was firmly stored in his memory.

The second part of my speech didn't go so well though. 'You also need to be prepared for his injury. Where they have removed the skull, his skin has sunk in.' They would all reply, 'I'll be fine, don't worry,' and every time they would all say after, 'Sorry. I thought I'd be prepared for that,' and then need to sit down or get some fresh air outside as they became teary-eyed. Paul would often pick up on this and would put his cap on. Although he wasn't totally back with us, he could sense people's emotions around him.

Paul's old sparring partner and good mate Mark Legge stayed in a hotel about five miles from the hospital for about a month. At this stage, Paul's short-term memory was already starting to show that it was not working properly.

A doctor could come in and have a conversation with Paul and then come back 20 minutes later and Paul would re-introduce himself to him. However, he remembered Mark and that he was at university and he would run from the hotel to the hospital and back.

The second Mark walked in he'd say, 'How did you do kid? What time did you do last night?' Mark was amazed.

Mark might have had something to do with the weight issue too. He used to sneak food past the doctors and nurses, bringing in bags of bananas, pints of milk and anything else he knew Paul liked.

Once, I walked in and they were having a feast. They were both digging into triple decker sandwiches and before I could say anything, Paul said, 'This is glorious. It's like being in five-star accommodation.'

He's a good lad Mark.

****

WITHIN a matter of weeks of Paul arriving at Castle Hill, they had him walking again. They did an incredible job. Although physically he was making good progress, his brain was all over the place and most of the time he thought he was in a hotel.

One time, he thought he was fighting later that night against Junior Jones.

Not a rematch, but the first time round. His brain was almost a year behind. Paul even said, as he pointed down the corridor, 'Take me to that room, my trainer is in there waiting for me.' The doctor had to wheel him in his chair there, just to show him he wasn't.

Other times, he would pack his bags and say, 'I'm leaving. I'm going.' I'm not even sure if he knew where or why, but I had to get the doctors and nurses to restrain him and bring him back. It was incredibly tough.

The problem was that Paul thought he could fight.

The doctor at Castle Hill had given me strict instructions not to say any different to him as that could have sent him into a serious panic. Instead, he would tell Paul when the time was right.

When that day came, he was quite blunt and told him it was over. Paul just had a vacant look on his face. It took him about a year to fully understand although he never really did accept it.

After a few weeks we were allowed to bring Paul home for a weekend to slowly get him used to his old surroundings. However, every time we did, he didn't want to go back to Castle Hill. He was getting frustrated and disorientated. A few days later I decided to have a chat with the doctor and said, 'I think he's alright to come home now. I'd like him to come home.'

The doctor looked at me and outlined the implications of this move. He told me, 'Mrs Ingle, you will, in essence, be Paul's full-time carer. Although he's made incredible progress, probably far more than many had predicted a couple of months ago, he's still very dependent. He's incontinent with urine at the moment, he needs help with washing and dressing and he needs constant reassurance. I just want to make sure you are mentally prepared for this.'

I replied instantly and unhesitatingly, 'He's my son. I'm his mother. Mothers look after their sons. I want him home.'

Two weeks later, after having spent five-and-a-half weeks at Castle Hill Hospital, Paul was home. I didn't want him being comfortable with those surroundings. It wasn't home and I wanted to make sure Castle Hill never felt like home to him.

****

I NEED to make a point of thanking Mr Battersby, his team and every one at Castle Hill.

They left no stone unturned, especially him – he saved my son's life. Over the weeks and months after Paul's operation, he was able to give me a clearer picture about Paul's injury, as he'd had time to look at the fight on DVD.

I was interested to know if the clot had been there beforehand and he was very honest when he said, 'It's hard to answer that question. It looks very unlikely that it occurred pre-fight.

'You can have situations where a small clot can have occurred sometime before and rebleeds, which is common in the elderly, but with Paul it's highly probable that the injury occurred as a result of one or more blows during the fight. Possibly the blows which brought him to his knees in round 11 were the ones which tore the veins. But I'm pretty certain that clot was not there at the beginning of the fight.

'If Paul wasn't fighting as he normally would, that could have been down to dehydration which might have resulted from a number of factors such as his extreme exercise regime, acute fluid loss or even something as simple as the heat of the spotlights in the ring.

'It's hard to determine an exact reason. All I can confirm is that the blood clot was fresh when I operated. It certainly didn't happen weeks or months before.'

It was hard to believe that three months had passed since Paul's fight with Botile. The journey which started off on the neurological ward, then moved to intensive care, a high dependency unit, a general ward and finally rehabilitation felt more like three years.

Each day, on occasions, felt like a month. Never once did that time feel shorter than it actually was.

Sadly, the next chapter in Paul's life would come with more challenges than he'd ever faced in the ring.

'Everybody gives you advice, but at the end of the day it's down to you. Learning to do everything from scratch again is demoralising. The worst part is that while you are trying to walk and eat again, the fire still burns deep inside and doesn't give you a break.'
- *Spencer Oliver, former European super-bantamweight champion and survivor of a blood clot on the brain*

Round 16

□

In a Negative Vacuum

(Paul Ingle continues his story)

MARK LEGGE came round to the house a few weeks after I came home and somehow managed to get me to do some light jogging. It was at a time when I kept saying no to everything, so it was quite an achievement.

We jogged for about a mile on the seafront and a few days later an article popped up in the *Scarborough Evening News* showing us running. My enthusiasm didn't last. What was the point? I had goals before.

I can't imagine I was much fun to be around for most people but, worst of all, I must have been a nightmare to my mum, the only person I really, totally trusted.

That still really upsets me – she supported me in everything and never left my side when I was in a coma. Now I was repaying her by being mean.

My brain was all over the place and, as well as the mood swings, I was also now getting increasingly paranoid. On one occasion, I'd got it stuck in my head that Ray Simpson was coming to the house and I told my mum, 'Don't let him come here, he'll tell me off. I've failed. I don't want to see him.' I then sprinted out of the back door and Kenny Brock had to chase me down to get me back in.

The truth is, if there was anyone who would never see me as a failure, it was Ray. He was like a father to me. When Ray found out, he was pretty tearful.

Four months after the accident, I had another problem to deal with. My appetite had become huge. I'd always had a good one but after the injury the part of my brain which was controlling things like hunger and how much I should be eating became affected.

Initially, nobody was getting too concerned. If anything they were happy to see me put some weight on after being seven stone soon after the op and the opposite, which could as easily have happened, would have been more of a worry.

In the boxing world, Botile lost his world title to my old sparring partner Frankie Toledo and then a few months later Manuel Medina knocked Frankie out in five rounds. To know I'd beaten or could beat these guys added to my growing frustration.

As 2001 started to unfold, my overall confusion was starting to clear up a little. A lot still didn't make sense and I was still trying to piece together what had happened, but I now realised I was, finally and definitely, out of boxing. I no longer thought I was back in the nineties and I was becoming more familiar with my surroundings.

Nine months after the Botile fight, Frank Maloney kindly organised a fundraiser for me. It was a football match between 'The Paul Ingle Squad' and *The Dream Team*, which was a massive series on television at the time, followed by an evening dinner. Testimonials don't tend to happen that often in boxing, so I felt honoured.

The opposition had about 15 players turn up, whereas my boys, managed by myself and Joe Royle, had over twice that. The number of boxers and stars who volunteered to play was incredible. I was genuinely touched.

My side included the likes of Glenn McCrory, Ricky and Matthew Hatton, Spencer Oliver and Julius Francis. It was unquestionably one of the toughest teams ever to walk onto a pitch, you wouldn't have wanted to face them.

The programme produced was about 40 pages long and unbelievable. Every major boxing writer around at the time wrote a tribute to me, wishing me the very best. Steve Bunce, Colin Hart, Claude Abrams, Colin McMillan and Steve Lillis penned beautiful pieces, which I appreciated enormously.

As much as I wanted to get into the spirit of things, I found it really difficult. Many people were asking me questions, to which I had to guess the answers to because my memory was shot and a number were trying to pick me up with motivational conversations which started to have the opposite effect after a while.

It was nobody's fault and I don't want to sound ungrateful after so many amazing people helped to make the evening happen and raise loads of money, but I simply wasn't comfortable. In fact, I don't think many of the boxers I was chatting to were either. There was a certain shyness about them and I could sense that they were struggling to know what to think and say.

Most of the players on my side were still involved in professional boxing. It was hard for me to see them out on the pitch when only a few months earlier I would have been there with them. As glad as I was with the money raised on the day, I just wanted my life back.

Many of my good mates also raised loads of cash for

the Royal Hallamshire Hospital neurological department. The likes of Mark Legge, Chris Hooper and Franny Norton all raised thousands for the place which had helped keep me alive.

I even got Mark some camouflage shorts and a vest and called him, 'The Running Hunter'. My mate Daz Smith, who absolutely hates running, joined over 50 others and piled into a big coach from Scarborough to take part in the Great North Run. I was very proud of all of them. I probably could have taken part in something if I'd had the motivation, but I didn't. I had nothing to spur me on.

****

ALMOST a year after the surgery, me and my mum had decided to go ahead with having a titanium plate fitted in my head as I couldn't go on with this gaping hole covered by only a flap of skin. I would have had it done earlier but the doctors said they needed to make sure I'd made sufficient progress first.

All operations do come with risk. We were told about the usual stuff like the possibility of infection but they also mentioned I could also have further memory loss and there would be a possibility that I might have another stroke. We weighed up the options and both came to the conclusion it was the right thing to do.

The operation took a whole day. I woke up about eight hours after surgery and the nurse and my mum were there looking at me. The nurse then asked, 'What's your name?' I replied, 'Paul Ingle.' She continued, 'Where do you live and what's your date of birth.' I got both of those questions right which is better than I would have done about four months earlier. It was a massive relief and, thankfully, there were never any effects.

The new titanium plate had been specially made by a dental technician to exactly match the piece of skull removed from my head. Not only was it lightweight, strong and wouldn't get infected, it was stronger than the original skull and would bounce back into shape it if was hit – which came in handy on a few occasions.

A few months afterwards, I slipped in the shower and banged my head on the bath. My mum came rushing upstairs in a mad panic and was on the phone to my brother straight away to take me to the hospital. I was actually very relaxed about the whole thing and was more worried I'd damaged the bath.

Dean drove us down to the hospital at high speed and we got an X-ray done straight away. Soon after, the nurse smiled and confirmed, 'That plate is stronger than the rest of his head, he's fine, his blood pressure is up a little bit though.' My mum said, 'So is mine.'

As the days, weeks and months passed, and even to this very day, I would often touch the plate and think to myself it feels strange. It's not a natural thing to have in your head and there's no feeling around it either. I doubt it will ever feel natural.

****

I WAS up and walking around pretty quickly after the operation and I felt like I needed to be as I'd now put on about four stone since the accident. The doctors reckoned it could have been some of the hormones in my body which were not working properly as a result of my injury, which contributed to the weight gain.

It was pretty demoralising as I couldn't train like I used to in order to take the weight off and I was also trying to eat far less and healthier. It felt like I was swimming against the tide.

Around this time, Steve Pollard kindly organised for me to be part of Chris Hooper's corner for his pro-debut in Hull. I'd known Chris since I was about 20. He'd moved up to Scarborough from London and we ended sparring together from my amateur days right through to my challenge against Medina for the world title. He's an absolutely lovely lad.

I didn't have an official role, I was there to help motivate Chris and shout instructions at him in between rounds from the ring apron. I advised him, 'Keep your head moving when you're against the ropes.' Or, 'Slip the jab, counter right hook.' Chris knocked out his opponent in the sixth round and then two months later in early 2002, he went on to win his second fight, also by stoppage.

After the second fight, Chris spoke to the crew from Sky Sports and said, 'It was an honour to have Paul in my corner. I'm unbeaten as a pro with him, so he's obviously bringing me good luck.'

He then came to me afterwards and said, 'Cheers for your continuing advice, all worked out well. You do know that the only reason Sky are here is because of you – don't you?' I thought he was being daft.

Unfortunately, it would be the last time I worked the corner with Chris. The truth is, I was starting to put more and more weight on and as much as I wanted to be involved in boxing, all I kept thinking about and finding increasingly difficult to come to terms with, was that I was only 29 and should have still been in the ring myself.

I was told by several well-meaning people that I was hitting a crossroads which all boxers reach after finishing in the sport. I couldn't accept it. The pathway had been forced on me and I had no idea of which road to take.

I ended up more and more frustrated and dropped deeper into depression. I started to attend fewer fights and turned down complimentary ringside tickets until I wasn't contacted anymore.

I hadn't fallen out of the circle, I'd decided to jump. It was almost as if I'd decided I was no longer Paul Ingle. The accident had changed me into a person I couldn't relate to anymore and, truthfully, one I couldn't cope with. I was a long way from accepting this version of me.

The rest of 2002 was a very mixed bag. Me and my fiancée split up which was very difficult to take as we had put in place wedding plans. My mum thankfully moved into my house to take care of me but, more than anything, I was starting to become a bit of a recluse.

The enquiry which the British Boxing Board of Control opened a few weeks after the fight had finally come through, with an offer which we accepted. They had originally offered me £10,000 for the injuries I'd suffered, but my mum replied back to them and said, 'He's worth more than that. He's got a disability now, he's brain damaged.' She was furious.

She took me to Leeds and got me assessed by an independent doctor who established, in addition to not being able to smell or taste at that point, I couldn't even stand on one leg. Soon after his report was sent off to the Board, we received a phone call to say I would be getting £50,000.

That money basically paid the mortgage off on the house. It didn't improve my quality of life but at least it gave me one less financial headache. I'd been within touching distance of having the rematch with Naz and becoming a multi-millionaire and here I was now on £50-a-week disability benefit and some compensation money. It was sickening.

Whilst my wedding dreams had gone up in smoke, my good mate Daz Smith was ready to tie the knot in the autumn. A few weeks before the big day, he knocked on my door and said he needed a favour from me. I was a little surprised as there was little I could do for myself at that point never mind anybody else.

He looked me straight in the eyes and said, 'Would you do me the honour of being my best man?' I was that shocked I didn't know what to say. Daz then said, 'You don't have to do a speech if you don't want to, I'd just be honoured for you to be there.' I was staggered and answered, with a smile on my face, 'Of course I'll do it. And I'll do a speech and let's not forget the stag do.'

We had a hug and it was a great moment. For the first time since the accident, I had something in front of me to genuinely focus on. With the help of my mum's best mate, Sandra Coole, who had been like an auntie to me ever since I was a kid, we sat down and wrote whatever dirt I could dish on Daz.

On the morning of the wedding, he came over to my house and my mum cooked us a massive breakfast before helping to get us both dressed. Daz is usually a very confident person but that morning he was a bag of nerves, literally shaking with them.

I had a chat with him and managed to calm him down a little bit and then my mum came over with a few glasses of champagne, which did the trick. We were ready to go and jumped into a lovely old Rolls Royce which was parked outside.

When it came to my turn to give the best man's speech, I was as nervous as hell. I'd spoken in front of thousands of people before but not since the accident. With over 100 there looking at me, I started and then froze straight away. I looked over at Sandra and she gave me a smile and a wink and I suddenly had my confidence back.

Although I lost where I was on the page on a few occasions, I managed to tell enough stories about Daz to get some laughs. At a time of my life when I was convinced I was good for nothing, this was a big achievement.

I got a huge round of applause and there were even a few tears of joy and the odd person standing up to clap. Daz was another who never gave up on me.

Just before Christmas, the council pulled down the remainder of the Edgehill estate. Although it was the right thing to do as vandals had started to set fire to most of the houses and cars on it, at a time when most of my memory still remained in the past, I felt like something important was being taken away from me. Something positive.

The pubs and social clubs disappeared and the community feel with it. The intention was to get rid of the guys who were causing problems but, instead, they came straight back and the majority of the other residents never did.

Since the accident, apart from the odd moment, I'd hated my last two years and wasn't looking forward to anything the future held.

****

THE horrible truth began starting to set in, I couldn't ignore it anymore. I'd only just turned 30 and the reality was I'd never fight again. I was talking, walking and feeding myself, which were three things which many thought I'd never do.

However, I wanted everything to be how it used to be, which simply wasn't realistic. When your aspirations and reality have no chance of meeting, it's the most demoralising thing in the world.

My goals before had been to fight for world titles. What did I have to aim for now? I wasn't going out, was sick of hearing advice, however well meaning, and rarely answered my phone or kept cancelling meet-ups. I'm surprised I have any friends left.

One thing all this did highlight was who my real friends were and who were the hangers on. On one occasion, my mum came back to the house really mad.

She told me, 'I was walking around town when a couple of your so-called mates called out from across the road, 'How's Paul doing?' I shouted back, 'Why don't you go to his house and see? You remember where he lives don't you? You were there to share in the glory, but not in the pain.' I told her not to get upset.

The fact is that they – and many others – never did come to the house and see me. The fact is they were never true friends.

The likes of Wayne, Daz, Kenny, Neil and many other close mates, after a while became immune to me pulling out after I'd agreed to meet up for a beer or go and watch the football down the pub and forgave me.

Occasionally I'd genuinely forgotten because of my short-term memory problems or I'd suddenly go off on one for no reason. Wayne once suggested about going training and I flipped, telling him, 'Who do you think you are telling me about training? I've done enough training in my life.'

It was almost as if I saw it all as a conspiracy. When my memory failed and I couldn't add up the pieces, I got suspicious and frustrated all at once. A lot of it made no sense to me and I'm sure not to everyone else.

The days, weeks and months ticked on and I continued to pile on more weight and do less exercise, letting life pass me by.

By 2005, the most eventful thing that had happened to me was being invited to the launch of the last Scarborough

Coal hump which, like the demolition of the Edgehill estate, was the closing of another chapter of my life.

In 2007, another benefit evening was kindly organised for me and once again I was staggered by the turnout from the general public and also the boxing fraternity. The likes of Steve Collins, Nigel Benn, Frank Maloney, Colin McMillan, Billy Hardy and my mate and top jockey Franny Norton all lent their support in my hometown of Scarborough.

Franny could have been a very good professional boxer. I first met him at the races in 1995 and had sparred with him on a few occasions. He was a very aggressive and powerful puncher who I'm sure would have won pro titles.

He won the stableboys championship eight times, boxed for England on many occasions and only lost one in over 50 amateur fights and that was against future professional European bantamweight champ, Ian Napa, in the ABA finals.

As with the earlier fundraiser, I was very grateful, but still very uncomfortable. I now weighed over 17 stone and was struggling to break a smile all night. Instead of seeing the positives, I just kept feeling everybody was giving me their pity.

For the next five years, I watched my life waste away. I'd put on so much weight, the size of the T-shirts I was wearing looked like a two-man tent hanging off me.

I was awarded the Freedom of the Borough of Scarborough in 2011 but I had nothing to be motivated about and was on a course of self-destruction. There was no way out. Not one that I could see anyway.

'**H**e fell from the very top and hit rock bottom and that is a long, long way down. He's been to hell and back, but his desire prevailed. That fighter's desire. He's proved himself to be a better fighter outside of the ring than he ever was inside it – and he was one hell of a world champion inside it.'
– Steve Collins, former super middleweight world champion

Round 17

□

The Eye of the Tiger

AS cheesy as it may sound, one of my favourite tunes to train to was 'Eye of the Tiger', from the film *Rocky III*. Maybe it's because it was from the era I grew up in, or that it was around the time when I started to win stuff as an amateur, but I loved training to that song. It used to set a little something off inside me that would make me want to train hard and go to my limit. I certainly hadn't had that feeling in a long time.

In the last *Rocky* movie, there's a scene where he speaks to his son and shakes him up with a powerful speech. 'It ain't about how hard you hit. It's about how hard you can get hit and how much you can take and keep moving forward.'

Sonny Pollard had sent me a message around the end of December 2012 saying he'd like to take me out for a bite to eat in early January, because he'd like to talk about organising a benefit dinner for me in May 2013.

I first met Sonny when I was 21 and he was 17, just before I was getting ready to turn pro with his dad. We sparred hundreds of rounds over the years and it was always a pleasure sharing a ring with him because he was always so eager to learn.

However, from about 2003 we hadn't seen each other a lot because he was going through some family and business problems and I'd lost the motivation to want to meet up with anyone. Sonny's always been a good mate and it didn't matter that we'd lost touch because the second we did hook up, it was as if we'd only seen each other a week before.

When he knocked on the door that January afternoon, I could see he looked a bit teary-eyed. Sonny had spotted how depressed I seemed and that I'd also ballooned in weight.

As I stepped into his car, I was very aware that Sonny could see I was really struggling to get my 21 stone gut through the door. I'm usually a very chatty sort of guy but on this occasion I didn't say a word as we drove a couple of miles into town.

The second we parked up, Sonny turned to me and asked, 'What's the matter Paul?' I'd normally say that it was nothing but I couldn't do that anymore. I felt comfortable opening up to Sonny and knew he wouldn't judge me, so I told him straight.

'If I can just get this fucking weight down, you'll see a different Paul Ingle. If I could start running again, you'll see a different Paul Ingle. Nothing seems to work – nothing. Everyone's trying to give me advice about training. Training – I was fucking world champion.

'I don't need their sympathy or advice. The fire to be involved in boxing still burns in my stomach, but there's nothing I can do with it. I used to be able to throw a ten-punch combination without hardly touching the floor, now I struggle to put a pair of shoes on. I don't want anybody to see me like this. I mean it Sonny – nobody.'

We sat there for about five minutes chatting and we were both pretty emotional. Sonny then gave me my *Rocky* talk and I'll never forget every last word of it.

He said, 'Paul, I couldn't give a shit if you were 30 stone as long as you are happy and content in yourself. You'll always be my mate and I'll always admire you for who you were and who you are now.

'What I do care about is that you look genuinely sad and that's a side I've never seen before. That's a side we need to make disappear. When you opened the door for me earlier, I had to fight back the tears seeing you so low.'

Sonny took a small breath and then shouted at me. 'You're a fucking double world champion Ingle! You brought the standard of boxing up in any gym you ever set foot in.

'When you became champion everybody wanted to be like you. Your love of boxing was contagious and you raised the bar in terms of commitment and dedication from the other fighters. And being selfish, if it wasn't for you Paul, I would have never fought on these big televised bills.

'Michael Watson had a similar end to his career, perhaps worse, and Gerald McClellan has been left blind, almost deaf and needs 24-hour care. But they continue to try and pull their lives back together.

'You can still do something with your life. If that fire still burns in your stomach, let's feed it. You don't need to box to be involved in boxing Paul. There's loads of other ways you can still be involved. I'm going to help you. I don't have a plan as yet but I'm not walking away from this, even if you tell me to fuck off.'

I had created a mental barrier that after a while became a stubborn pride thing. I had held on to the grief, pain and mental scars of the Botile fight for so long that it was almost as if I was stuck in the year 2000. Now was the time to break free. There's an old expression, 'If the head is not fit, the body will follow.' It was time to get positive.

A few days later, Sonny knocked on the door and we sat down for a cup of tea. I was determined to let him tell me his plan.

He mentioned that he wanted to get me back in the public eye again. He wanted to help answer the question, 'Whatever happened to Paul Ingle?' By getting the press involved, not only would they see what a state I'd become, but they'd be able to track my progress.

I told him that I wasn't sure about that, how I was almost scared to pick up a copy of a paper and read an article about myself because it would show a picture of me bursting out of a XXXXL T-shirt and the article would always be very negative.

Sonny said, 'Journalists can only write about what's in front of them. It's time to give them something positive to write about.' I liked the sound of that.

I replied, 'I'm tired of people making comments about how fat I am and hearing when walking down the streets of Scarborough, 'Is that Paul Ingle the former world champion? Look at the size of him.' Then two seconds later they say, falsely, 'Hi champ, you look well.'

Sonny had already been hard at work and in touch with Ed Robinson from Sky Sports and also Daniel Gregory of the *Scarborough Evening News,* to make sure everyone knew what I was up to. Daniel especially has been outstanding, willing to write a piece on me with a moment's notice and travel to a media launch irrespective of distance.

Sonny mentioned that it was about time I got my life story written. I wasn't sure but the more I thought about, the more going over my life and piecing it back together was going to be a help.

Then, he talked about the subject which was making me the most nervous. This was the thing I was convinced he would not be able to repair or make any impact on – my weight.

Over the years, doctors gave me different diets to follow and even tablets, but nothing made a dent. I had followed everything exactly as I was told and in those early days was even walking a few miles, determined to shift the weight.

Sonny then explained his plan. He'd been chatting with a guy called Alex Hall and had mentioned to him that he was looking for a diet for me. Alex told Sonny that he'd just invested into something called Herbalife and talked about the benefits of it.

He explained that you don't just drink a shake and you lose ten stone – a disciplined lifestyle and diet would need to work with it, then you would see the effects. I liked the sound of 'discipline' again. I'd based my whole life around it as a boxer and felt that could be the focus I was looking for.

I officially started the diet in April 2013. Unfortunately, the stuff did not come free and Alex knew I wasn't rolling in cash, so he kindly paid for my first month. A month later, it was as if Sonny's plan suddenly went into overdrive.

The fundraiser which he and Dean Hoggard organised for me not only happened but was a great success. Kell Brook, Spencer Oliver and loads of other people from the boxing world lent their support yet again, not to mention Tony Armstrong from Napoleon's casino who sponsored the whole event.

The other major triumph, although it wasn't instantly recognisable, was the fact that I'd lost 15lbs in just one month. The diet worked. Although people were still staring that

239

night at the size of my gut, I felt better in myself. I knew I'd lost weight and knew that more was going to come off.

The funds raised from the evening helped to pay for about another five months of the diet and by the time I'd finished the course, I was down to 17 stone. When Sonny came around, we looked at an old picture of me five months earlier. Then, I had no neck and I was leaning back leading with my stomach as I walked. I looked like a cartoon character.

It looked like somebody had taken a picture from my world title days and done a caricature of what I'd look like fat. We both managed to laugh about it and that was a great motivation to continue.

I was over the moon. I kid you not, it was as if somebody had hit play for the 'Eye of the Tiger' soundtrack. Although I wasn't quite ready to start punching beef or chasing chickens, everything Sonny was promising was coming true and I felt so much better in myself.

My diet had now become routine. Breakfast would consist of a shake, multivitamins and protein tablets, lunch was the same and tea-time would be a full meal, like a chicken or turkey salad, but again with the vitamins and protein tablets.

If I wanted a little snack in between meals, it would be something like a piece of fruit. Now and then I allowed myself a cheat meal such as lovely Chinese, but that would only happen about once every six weeks.

It wasn't just about the weight though. Mentally I was getting stronger with every pound I was losing. I was now getting out in town more and when people said, 'You're looking well,' I genuinely knew they meant it. Obviously, some people were still making whispered comments about me being fat but I'd say to myself, 'I'll show you.'

I'd lost over four stone in six months by this point but

was also very aware that the cash from the fundraiser had just about finished. Sonny then gave me a buzz to let me know some more good news.

He'd found private sponsors who were going to pay for the diet until another sponsor took over. I asked who they were, but he just said, 'Private sponsors, Paul. Nothing for you to worry about.' For almost the next year, 'they' made sure my supplements were there for me and by February 2014, I'd dropped even more weight, bringing me down to 16 stone.

The weight loss was perfect timing as I was about to go in front of the Sky Sports television cameras. Sonny had pulled together an incredible amount of resources and energy to launch the 'Paul Ingle Boxing Academy' in a very short space of time. This wasn't part of the original plan of me getting my life back together but it was yet another incredible thing he had done for me.

Sonny picked me up in the morning and we drove to the academy in Hull. As we pulled up outside the gym doors, there was a 20-foot sign which had a picture of me in the middle, I couldn't believe it.

Sonny turned to me and said, 'This is in your honour, Paul. You trained here for pretty much most of your professional career, so even when you are not in the gym, people will still feel your presence.'

As I stepped out of the car, I instantly realised that the academy was located right in the middle of a tough estate where quite a few people were doing drugs or swigging from a can of strong beer in broad daylight.

Many of my mates who I grew up with on the Edgehill estate are either dead from drugs and booze, or behind bars. Very few people who stepped into Scarborough Amateur Boxing Club followed that route, though.

The academy will give people from all backgrounds the opportunity to choose a different path in life and, you never know, from that estate a world champion may emerge. Stranger things have happened.

As I stepped inside, ex-champ Jamie Moore and Daniel Gregory greeted me before we started to film a short programme for Sky. My nephew Harry had also come up and to have the opportunity to work the pads with him in the ring, in a place with my name over the door, was simply astonishing. I suddenly had reason and value.

The future plans are to get the academy ABA-affiliated and for it to get not-for-profit status. Sonny's also hoping to design a Paul Ingle boxing trainer's college course, which would allow people to gain an NVQ Level 3 and would help them to get a job at a fitness centre or the like.

****

THREE months later, Sonny had yet more good news. He'd found a new sponsor for my diet which would take me into the summer of 2015. Apart from being a weight off my gut, it was also a big one off my mind.

Although Sonny never wanted me to know, a little birdie told me who the 'private sponsors' were. Sonny and a great guy called Dean Hoggard took over the payment of the Herbalife after the money from the benefit evening ran out.

I know for a fact that Sonny was virtually broke and going through a bad stage in his life at this point, so to drop about two grand between the supplements and travelling up and down to see me during those months was more than an incredible gesture. He never told me because he never wanted me to feel I owed him. It's not about the money, but I don't think I'll ever be able to repay his generosity.

My new sponsor is a lad called Lee Stephenson who works for Herbalife. Sonny introduced me to him in May 2014 and we hit it off straight away. Lee explained how he intended to work with me and also outlined that he wasn't just here to pay for my supplements, he genuinely wanted to help me reach my target of 11-12 stone.

Although I'd been using the diet, up to that point, I didn't really have anybody working with me to make sure I was doing it properly. Me and mum would measure my weight every few weeks but with it dropping off far slower than before, it was great timing to have Lee on board to guide me through the difficult or more stubborn part of the rest of my weight loss.

Lee explained to me that the diet would give me all the essential nutrients I'd need to keep my body going but I couldn't just sit on that all my life. In order to get the best out of it, I'd need to live a more active lifestyle. It all made perfect sense.

He told me straight, 'I'll be coming up to see you once a month and I'll be asking you what exercise you've done. Each time I'll be expecting to see progress. If you tell me you've been for a 30-minute walk, I'll be very happy, but next time I'll be expecting at least 35 minutes.

'I'll also be weighing you and doing a fat test. You keep saying you want to start running again, well here are the first steps to getting you there.' It was just what I needed to hear and the timing was perfect.

A month after starting my regime with Lee, another milestone happened, again, thanks to Sonny. l was presented with an award from the WBC, who recognised my contribution to boxing and, that if it wasn't for my accident, I would have certainly challenged for their belt, probably against Naz.

The Yorkshire Hunter

The charitable arm of the WBC – World Boxing Cares – gave me their ambassador award and it was presented by David Walker and none other than former dual weight world champion, Steve Collins. The recognition meant a lot to me but, more than anything, I was getting back into boxing, something I had decided to turn my back on for nearly a decade.

****

THE weight is still coming off, I'm now a little over 14 stone and enjoying knuckling down to the challenge ahead of me. Friends and family have started to say how my voice sounds a lot more like it used to when I was boxing and my good looks are also returning. I had a genuine concern that as I lost weight, the plate in my head would become more prominent.

That truth is, it has become far less visible than before. As my head started to get fatter, the plate became more and more indented and was gaining more attention. Nowadays, I look in the mirror and give it a tap, but I do so with a smile. It's part of me, whether it looks good or bad. I needed to accept that and I have.

Now I have a system I can see works, I'm willing to put in the time and effort to reach my target weight. I have belief in it. It's not about starving yourself, that makes you miserable and I've gone through enough of that.

I want to enjoy this and I'm not going to give up. I did give up on a lot of things that had been important to me and it led to a downward spiral of feeling even worse.

It won't happen overnight, but if you start to make those small changes, you'll never regret it. If somebody was to tell me they have fish and chips every day for supper, I'd tell them to run to the shop instead of driving! There are always ways to burn more calories in your daily routine.

I used to sweat buckets walking up the stairs to go to the loo. Nowadays, it will take a decent walk to do that – I'm getting fitter and leaner.

Like with the time with Neil Featherby in the US when I imagined I was drinking a pint of beer, I now call my supplement my steak and veg. When it comes to my evening meal, my tastebuds are going through the roof and I can't wait to dig into my salad. Everything you eat has so much more flavour because you appreciate it that much more.

Dieting is harder than fighting. I've been at this longer than any training camp, and there's no big glory parade at the end or any belt to be won. The prize comes by way of feeling great. The fight I have now is with myself and I'm coming through. I gave up but now the Hunter is back.

'**P**aul goes everywhere
with me and Harry and
follows his amateur
boxing very closely. Harry's
only just turned 12, and is just
starting to understand just
how good his uncle was.
I started to show him videos of
Paul boxing. He now very
proudly says to everyone,
'That's my uncle Paul. He was
world champion."
                    - *Dean Ingle, Paul's brother*

Round 18

☐

Bearing No Grudges

MY short-term memory after the Botile fight hasn't been great. When getting this book together, my mum has been a great help reminding me of certain events. When she talked about them it was the first time she'd done so in such detail and she was fantastic. I sat there watching her well up as the truth was painfully recalled.

She recounted being told the initial prognosis from Robert Battersby and was talking about him finding something when they removed part of the skull. I interrupted and said, 'Was there something in there?'

She looked puzzled at first and said, 'Yes, it was a clot,' thinking I had totally forgotten about the operation.

I then said, 'Oh, I thought you meant he had found a brain.' She suddenly realised that I had just made a joke about a subject I had never wanted to talk about. We laughed together and it was an important moment to share.

She's able to laugh with me because she realises again how comfortable I've become with myself, slowly but surely accepting my limitations.

My mum has also become very protective over the years and I've now been confident enough to tell her that, on a number of fronts, I really am ok. With part of my peripheral vision in my left eye gone, whenever we walk around town, she walks on my left side, worried that I won't see people and bump into them.

She has taken charge of my care for most of the last 15 years. Although I've improved vastly since then, she's had her work cut out on occasions and she's never complained once. She sacrificed a job, a social life and many other things which I'll never know about. She is my best friend, my parent and my inspiration. My template of how to live when the chips are down has been right there in front of me since the day I was born.

With my self-esteem higher than it's been for a long time, I think I'm ready for a holiday abroad and I'd like to treat my mum – although I did try and organise one a couple of years after coming out of hospital.

I knew she didn't want to fly but I thought that if I got her a passport, she might change her mind. I filled out the forms with some help from a friend, popped in a photo of her, signed the forms and then a few weeks later, it arrived in the post but she still refused. The passport never got used and has now expired, but it was worth a try.

****

ONE of the most common questions I've been asked since the Botile fight, which I feel better placed to answer now is, should boxing be banned?

Absolutely not. Boxing has been my life since I was a seven-year-old kid. Everybody runs a risk in whatever they do. I knew them when first entering a ring.

There's a ref in the ring and we are wearing gloves. It's not a street fight with baseball bats and knuckle dusters. The number of people who end up with brain injuries, or suffer death in boxing is minimal compared to many other sports which never seem to have this debate raised.

It's the toughest sport but I would never turn my back on it. It was my life and always will be. I don't need to be fighting in a ring anymore to be involved in boxing and I'm starting to see all the other rewarding ways I can still keep myself tied to it.

Banning boxing would force it to go underground. What I would like to see is the safety of the fighters and the sport in general improving – like in Formula One. As the cars got faster over the years, the risk increased for the drivers. So much time, effort, money and expertise has been put into making F1 safe, especially after Ayrton Senna's fatal crash in 1994.

When Spencer Oliver's accident happened, many people said it was just lucky that he had the right people around him and he was moved quickly to hospital. Including Spencer, myself and other boxers who have suffered brain injuries, I'm sure there's enough experience to write up a procedure which outlines exactly who and what is needed should a head injury occur.

Luck should play no part but a thorough examination of what is needed to take a brain injury from the ring through to the surgeon as safely and quickly as possible.

Who is to say but, maybe, in the future a portable, wireless hand-held CT scanner might be invented which could be pointed at a fighter's head like a barcode scanner at a supermarket, so they can be instantly checked between each round.

Having a neurosurgeon present at fights would also

be ideal. Having the right knowledge, technology and skills ringside could mean the difference between life and death. All these things will add additional costs but if it potentially saves lives, surely it's worth it.

One of the areas of boxing which definitely needs to be sorted out, is dehydration. The way I dropped weight for the Jones fight was perfect. Neil Featherby had it down to a sweet science. Unfortunately, for the Botile fight, the amount of weight I lost and the way I did it, in a short time frame, was a disaster.

For me, the issue here is not so much who is responsible for sensible weight loss, it's what measures are in place to make sure a boxer does it sensibly. A checking system that would not allow the boxer to fluctuate so dramatically in between fights would be ideal.

Dehydration is not something new but it certainly needs more research done to help professional athletes pushing themselves to their limits.

Whatever future studies are done to help with that issue in boxing could be used for other sports and vice versa. Take, for example, my jockey mate, Franny Norton. He's perhaps unique in so much as he's been a boxer before jumping on a horse.

Indeed, the pressures of making weight for jockeys are even worse, because it's probably the only sport in the world where they need to be bang on almost every day of the year.

When speaking to Franny recently, he mentioned that a university study had just been done which looked at the challenges involved with jockeys making the weight. One of the interesting things they found out was that it could be achieved by concentrating more on reducing body fat and without having to starve or sweat as much. I'm sure boxing already takes this on board, but if there are any golden nuggets of information out there to apply in similar situations, it can only help.

****

COMING to terms with not being able to fight again was, possibly, the hardest adjustment in my life.

I didn't feel resentful about my accident initially because the implications didn't really set in for a few years. The more I remembered and added up, the more frustrated I became. I wanted to turn the clock back and make up for lost time, and refused to see why that wasn't possible.

As much as I tried to turn off the boxing side of my brain, it would always instinctively turn itself on. Even at my lowest, when the boxing came on the television, I'd suddenly find myself shouting, 'slip the jab,' or, 'cover up.'

If my friends and family were round at the time and they'd hear me doing the live commentary, they'd say, 'Go down the boxing club, Paul. You've got loads to offer.'

By about 2007, I started to hide behind the same excuse, 'I'm going to apply for a coaching badge once I've lost this weight,' or 'I'll also start going down the gym again once I've lost this weight.' It was never going to happen, though. How could I preach to impressionable youngsters about looking after and taking care of themselves when I clearly couldn't? Instead I used to just sit on the sofa and waste away.

When Sonny came to me with his plan of how to get my life back, it was like I'd been in hibernation for ten years. I've now accepted I'm not fighting anymore but I've also realised that I genuinely do have something to offer in boxing; my knowledge.

It's the nearest substitute for being in the ring as a fighter and boxing runs through my veins. It's what has taken me down, but it's also what will bring me back up. Without boxing I'd be a lost soul. That's why it's essential for me to keep in touch with boxers and all the other people involved in the sport.

One thing I prided myself on throughout my boxing career was my boxing brain.

Steve Pollard once, kindly, said in an interview, 'Ingle had the heart of a lion and the brain of a professor.' I never once wanted to blast an opponent out of the ring, instead I always looked to systematically take them to pieces. Whatever has gone from my memory, it's certainly not my boxing brain. I feel I have a lot to pass on.

I'd also like to be able to guide boxers through the minefields outside of the ring. I had real issues with moving away from Scarborough during training camps simply because I felt relaxed with familiar surroundings. However, there are always small distractions in your own backyard, which don't seem like much but which, over time, will add up, whether it be going down the social club to have a game of snooker or playing a game of football when, perhaps, it would have been better resting for the day ahead.

I had good people around me to guide me how to eat, sleep and train but I didn't always listen to them. It's also vital to identify your hangers-on from the early stages. The group will only get bigger and most of the time they are just in it for two things, money and fame.

Most of it you can figure out yourself but there's no harm in getting guidance when you are unsure. Just pick your teachers wisely. I was lucky to have some great ones over the years.

****

ONE thing that has never changed is my welcome at Scarborough Amateur Boxing Club. It's now run by John Brownlie and I was over the moon to see that there's now a big sign outside saying, 'The Tommy Johnson Boxing and Fitness Centre'. A well-deserved credit to a man who guided me as an amateur and provided dreams, confidence and direction to so many people.

Thankfully the Ingle boxing blood runs through the family veins and there are currently two of my cousins and a nephew who are boxing there. I've hardly missed a single fight of theirs, even when I was at my lowest ebb and putting a pair of shoes on was a struggle.

George Ingle has had his fair share of success as an amateur boxer in over 60 fights, including reaching the ABA semi-finals. I bought him his first-ever gumshield when he was only six and I was getting ready to fight Colin McMillan for the British title.

When I had my accident, instead of turning away from boxing, George decided he wanted to be even more involved. Despite his mum saying she didn't want him to, especially after what had happened to me, he turned to her and said, 'He's my idol mam. I want to achieve what he did.'

George could make a great pro. He fights at lightweight and glides around the ring, dare I say, possibly better than me. On top of all that he packs a solid punch.

My other cousin Jamie Scotter, is a year older than George and they used to spar a fair bit and travel the amateur circuit together around England. Jamie, like George could certainly make a career out of the noble art. He's had over 90 amateur fights and won far more than he's lost.

My young nephew Harry is already showing all the

signs of turning into something special. I've only missed one of his amateur fights and whenever I have the chance, I go and see him train at Scarborough ABC. He's already got superb footwork and I've advised him on how to make it that little bit better. On numerous occasions he's heard me say, 'Get in and out. Don't leave your head in there.'

I'm normally quite a reserved guy, but when I'm ringside for Harry's fights, I'm screaming and shouting commands at him and giving him encouragement. When he's in the ring, I feel like I'm in there with him. I get butterflies in my stomach and the atmosphere gives me a real buzz.

Harry gives me a great sense of pride. Whenever we go to a show, he wants to introduce me to all his friends as a world champion. I now like saying, 'This is my nephew Harry – he's going to be world champion.'

****

FINALLY, I've got my boxing coach's licence. It's something I'd been promising to do for a long time and it's happened. At the end of 2014 I was in the corner for all nine of the lads fighting for Scarborough ABC, which was a real honour – and Harry and Jamie were two of them.

On the 20th December 2014, at the City Hall, Hull, Sonny Pollard made his comeback in the pro ring challenging for a Masters title against a lad called Danny Brown. I was there by the stool and it meant everything to me.

It's not that I'll ever be able to pay Sonny back for everything he's done for me, but to have the opportunity to be in his corner for that fight was the closest I could do. Although he lost the bout 79-75, he left everything in the ring that night and nobody was more proud than me of walking him into the ring and having the honour of hugging him at the end of the fight. To top it off, just when I thought my duties were over for the evening, I was asked to present the title belt to Danny, which was another honour.

The reception I was given as I was announced into the ring to make the presentation was immense. It was as if I'd been transported back in time, as the hair-raising chants of 'Innnnnnngle' started.

The boxing fraternity never abandoned me after my accident and it became so evident that night. I have many new journeys ahead of me and exciting things to learn and teach about the sport I love.

****

WRITING a book is a great experience but it's also an opportunity to put down things you might not always feel comfortable saying to someone face to face. In print you get the chance to pick the right, appropriate words and that is priceless.

After the Botile fight I was very saddened to hear how many people have never been the same again. It is time for all of us to move on. I've done enough of feeling low in the last 14 years and to hear that the people who helped me become world champion, and supported me along that route, have also suffered similar sadness, is heartbreaking.

Steve Pollard, Kellie Maloney and Neil Featherby have all said that never a day passes, when they don't think about that last fight and that they all feel a certain level of guilt.

I'd much rather you remembered only the previous 24 fights, the press conferences with horses bolting off, planes almost crashing on the way to New York and some of the best parties known to man. Not to mention picking up the British,

The Yorkshire Hunter

Commonwealth, Intercontinental, European, IBF and IBO world titles along the way. There's more than enough good times to concentrate on there.

I want to say, here and now, I hold nothing but love and respect for you all. Life is too short and, for a moment, on the 16th December 2000, life was almost over for me. I'm still standing and getting on with my life so if you want to do anything now, show me how proud you are, not pity or tears. I need your smiles and positivity. Without you all, a lot of what I achieved would have never happened. I owe you.

Lastly, I send out a message to Mbulelo Botile.

Me and you lived and died by the same code of honour. If there is someone who needs to hear these words, it's you. I don't need to forgive you for anything because you did nothing wrong.

We both knew the risks stepping through those ropes. I know you had a 21-year-old uncle called Lumkile Dunjana who died in the ring in 1967 fighting Anthony Sithole for the South African bantamweight title, that pain must have felt like it was coming back to haunt you.

I need to let you know that I'm not here to haunt you, I'm here to liberate you. We achieved what many people dream of – we both became champions of the world. Nobody can ever take that away from us.

You need to get on with your life and make it the best you can. If you ever make your way to Scarborough, look me up. I'll be the first person to shake your hand.

****

ONE of the most important people I had the pleasure of contacting when getting my book together was my brain surgeon, Mr Battersby.

The last time I'd spoken to him was in 2002, when I returned to the Royal Hallamshire Hospital to do some press for a new hi-tech MRI scanner.

He has saved a great number of lives and performed thousands of operations so it's essential he doesn't get close to his patients. If he was ever to develop an emotional bond with any of them, it could affect his judgement. That's why, like me with my jab, he always kept me at arm's length.

When asking him to help with this, I got the chance to simply say, 'Thank you.' It wasn't much more than that but I don't think it needed to be as he knew what I meant. Somehow, I managed to get the conversation on to boxing and asked him if he'd been interested in it before operating on me. His reply put a smile on my face.

He told me, 'I'm not interested in sport in general really. When I was at school in 1963, aged about 12, we were pressurised to take part in a boxing match. It wasn't compulsory, but it was what you were expected to do. I said I didn't want to box, it was a barbaric sport.

'The other kids started to call me a chicken and a coward, and so I decided to fight. I think they were matches of three rounds, three minutes long, which seemed forever. I won my weight division and the house I was representing got awarded the Strafford Boxing Cup.

'I thought to myself that's the end of that, when a catch-22 came up. If you won your weight division, you then had to box for the school, there was no way out of it. I carried on boxing until I was 16 and had about 20 fights in all, never losing any, except the last one.

'It was at Ipswich Naval College and I was fighting their captain, who was a tough lad. I was clearly outclassed. I can recall entering the ring and then all I remember after that was waking up about 30 minutes later by a swimming pool outside. I'd been knocked out in the first round. After that concussion I never boxed again.'

I was stunned, my brain surgeon not only a life saver but a good boxer in his day. The world could do with a lot more like him.

With help from the likes of Mr Battersby and my true mates and family, overall, I'm doing much better. The stroke which affected my arm still gives me a bit of bother with pins and needles but every year I seem to be getting stronger and more able to use it. My mood swings are far less frequent and I repeat myself and slur less than I used to.

One thing that makes me very happy now is to see my mum smiling more. She used to collect every newspaper article throughout my boxing career and made two huge scrapbooks. That stopped on the 16th December, 2000.

As a result of getting my life together once more, she's started to save those clippings again. To see my mum happy, not just for me, but in herself is worth more than all the money on the planet.

As for me, my ambition, from as long as I can remember, was to be the kid from the Edgehill estate who took on the world – and won. I reckon I did just that.

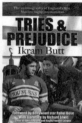

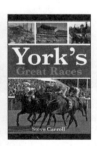

Funny Bones

My Life in Comedy

By Freddie 'Parrotface' Davies

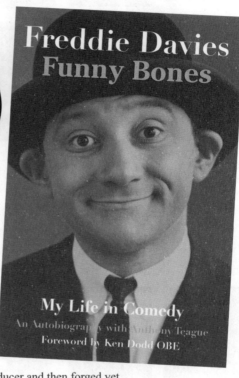

Freddie Davies
Funny Bones

My Life in Comedy
An Autobiography with Anthony Teague
Foreword by Ken Dodd OBE

In 1964, a single appearance on TV talent show *Opportunity Knocks* made 'Parrotface' comedian Freddie Davies famous overnight. Spectacular success followed, stars such as Judy Garland, Cliff Richard, even Cary Grant, were fans...

But when it all began to slip in the 1980s, Freddie became a producer and then forged yet another career as a serious actor. He appeared to great acclaim in a Royal Shakespeare Company production of *The Secret Garden* and cult film *Funny Bones* - alongside Lee Evans and Jerry Lewis - based on tales of Freddie's music hall comic grandfather Jack Herbert. Now he has come full circle, delighting audiences again as Samuel Tweet in theatres up and down the land.

Fifty years on from his television debut, Freddie finally tells his own story, revealing for the first time the tragedy behind his early days in Salford and a family secret that rocked his world. He paints a vivid and hilarious picture of a gruelling apprenticeship in the Northern clubs - revealing how 'Parrotface' spluttered into life.

With a foreword by the legendary Ken Dodd, this unique autobiography is a poignant and hilarious evocation of a vanished world, offering insights into the art of stand-up and a richly nostalgic treat for comedy connoisseurs.

Available in hardback or paperback

Just what *is* Yorkshireness...?

Yorkshire ... God's Own County ... The Broad Acres ... the Texas of England ... home to some of the UK's most captivating landscapes, coastlines, food, literature, history, music, tea, film, sport and beer, when Britain's largest county and its residents get you in their grip, you are unlikely to escape soon.

Venue for Le Grand Départ of 2014's Tour de France and voted the Leading Tourist Destination in Europe - beating off the challenges of Paris, Rome, London (ha!) and Vienna - the White Rose county is on the rise. *Slouching Towards Blubberhouses* is a timely and comical look at a region that is by turns friendly, uncompromising, boastful, blunt and maddeningly self-aware, from the viewpoint both of its chosen ones, who wouldn't live anywhere else, and those who look on in envy - or irritation - from outside.

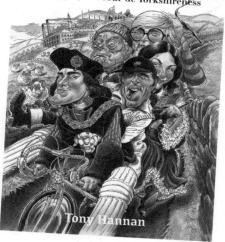

It delves beneath the eeh bah gum clichés of whippets, clogs, flat caps and moth-eaten wallets to explore what really makes Tykes tick. And it wonders if coming from Yorkshire still means owt in a changing and diverse 21st century.

Slouching Towards Blubberhouses

- A (right grand) Tour de Yorkshireness

By Tony Hannan

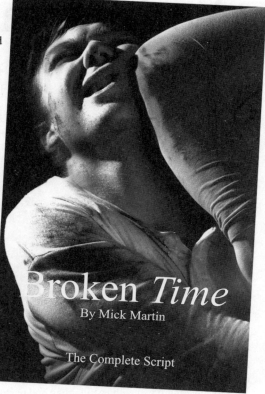

The Barefoot Shepherdess

and Women of the Dales

By Yvette Huddleston & Walter Swan

The Barefoot Shepherdess and Women of the Dales celebrates the variety and versatility of a dozen or more determined women who have made a distinctive life for themselves 'far from the madding crowd'.

The Yorkshire Dales attracts tourists aplenty to appreciate the beauties of the local landscape but most visitors return to their towns and cities, renewed by the peace and quiet of the countryside, though unable to leave their modern, urban lifestyle for too long.

Women like Alison O'Neill, who owns her own flock of sheep and designs her own brand of tweed clothing, demonstrate that you can live a life of independence and fulfilment even in Britain's remotest regions. There are inevitable hardships to be endured but innumerable compensations when the Dales are on your doorstep.

Each chapter features inspirational women who have made the choice to live and work collaboratively with the people and places of the Yorkshire landscape. What they have in common - farmers, artists, vets, publicans, entrepreneurs, artisans, academics, curators and vicars - is a passion for life where Yorkshire countryside and community coincide.

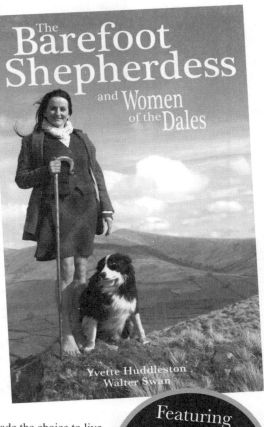

Featuring personalities from the ITV series **The Dales**

THE STORY OF FOOTBALL:

via the Moors, Dales and Wolds of England's largest and proudest county

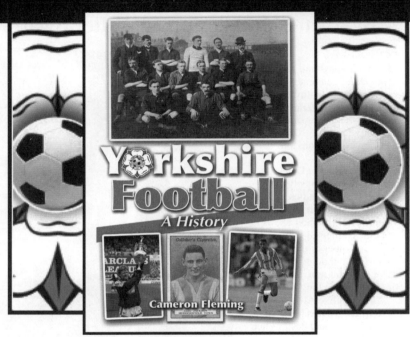

YORKSHIRE FOOTBALL - A HISTORY

 Cameron Fleming

ISBN: 978-0956252654

Scratching Shed Publishing Ltd

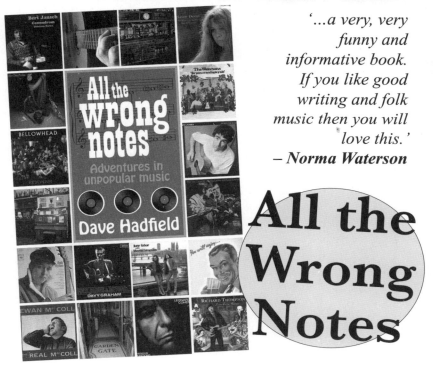

Adventures in Unpopular Music
By Dave Hadfield

For almost 50 years, Dave Hadfield has followed the genres of music that grabbed his youthful heart and mind. Now, in ALL THE WRONG NOTES, he has written not just a musical memoir, but a personal and social history of the last half-century. Like a Zelig with a finger in his ear, he has been where folk music has happened and describes it, affectionately but warts-and-all, in a way it has never been described before.

Hadfield's sure ear for quirks and eccentricities produces unique takes on major figures like Bob Dylan, Ewan MacColl and Leonard Cohen. It celebrates the foot-soldiers and their role in keeping left-field music alive. Humorous and provocative in equal measure, ALL THE WRONG NOTES is the key to a fascinating world of music.

Investigate all our other titles and
stay up to date with our latest releases at
www.scratchingshedpublishing.co.uk